AIA Guide
to Downtown
Minneapolis

Publication of the

AIA Guide to Downtown Minneapolis

has been made possible

through generous gifts from

AIA Minnesota
A Society of The American Institute of Architects

John R. Camp

George A. MacPherson Fund

Elmer L. and Eleanor Andersen Fund

Bean Family Fund for Business History

North Star Fund of the Minnesota Historical Society

Larry Millett

AIA Guide to Downtown Minneapolis

Minnesota Historical Society Press

www.mhspress.org

The Minnesota Historical Society Press is a member of the
Association of American University Presses.

10 9 8 7 6 5 4 3 2 1

International Standard Book Number
ISBN-13: 978-0-87351-720-1 (paper)
ISBN-10: 0-87351-720-2 (paper)

Library of Congress Cataloging-in-Publication Data
Millett, Larry, 1947–
    AIA guide to downtown Minneapolis / Larry Millett.
        p.   cm.
Includes bibliographical references and index.
        ISBN-13: 978-0-87351-720-1
        ISBN-10: 0-87351-720-2
    1. Architecture—Minnesota—Minneapolis—Guidebooks.
    2. Minneapolis (Minn.)—Buildings, structures, etc.—Guidebooks.
    3. Minneapolis (Minn.)—Guidebooks.
    I. Title.   II. Title: American Institute of Architects guide to
downtown Minneapolis

NA735.M5M48   2010
720.9776'579—dc22

                                                    2009007477

Front cover: Stone Arch Bridge and Minneapolis skyline, Hennepin
Avenue Bridge, and Foshay Tower reflection, all by Brian M. Gardner;
Hennepin Center for the Arts by Colleen McGuire; Flour Exchange
detail by Brian M. Gardner

Back cover: Minneapolis Public Library interior by Pete Sieger; Mill City
Museum from Minnesota Historical Society collections; Wells Fargo
Building detail by Brian M. Gardner

Contents

Symbols Used in this Guidebook

! A building or place of exceptional architectural and/or historical significance

N Individually listed on the National Register of Historic Places or included within a National Register Historic District

★ A building or place that has been designated as a National Historic Landmark

Ĭ A structure that has been designated as a Historic Civil Engineering Landmark

L Locally designated as a historic property or within a local historic district

i A property in which all or part of the interior is included within local historic designation

Abbreviations Used for Select Architectural Firms

ESG Architects	Elness, Swenson Graham Architects
HGA	Hammel, Green and Abrahamson
KKE Architects	Korsunsky Krank Erickson Architects
MS&R Architects	Meyer, Scherer and Rockcastle Architects
SOM	Skidmore, Owings and Merrill (Chicago)

Author's Note: This book is a revised, updated, and slighly expanded version of the chapters devoted to downtown Minneapolis in my *AIA Guide to the Twin Cities*, published in 2007. Some entries here appear exactly as they are in that book; others have been changed to reflect new information or to provide additional historic background. I have also added a number of entries for buildings that either were omitted from the *AIA Guide* because of space limitations or have been built since its publication.

Minneapolis Downtown

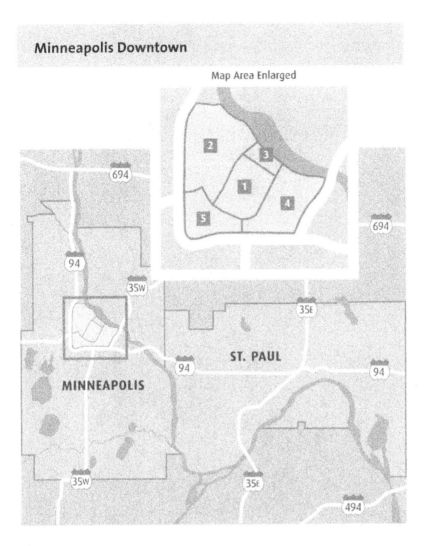

Map Area Enlarged

1 The Central Core
2 Hennepin Avenue and the Warehouse District
3 The Central Riverfront
4 Downtown East and Elliot Park
5 Loring Park

AIA Guide
to Downtown
Minneapolis

Overview

Downtown Minneapolis has the broad, spacious feel common to midwestern prairie cities. Its wide streets—measuring 80 to 100 feet across—are arranged in a standard gridiron of square blocks, and there are no bluffs or deep valleys to provide a sense of containment. Walk out onto a street in the middle of downtown, and you are in a world that looks as though it could go on forever. Downtown Minneapolis is well defined vertically, however, by the giant crop of skyscrapers that clusters near its center and serves as a potent symbol of the city's wealth and prestige.

As it's evolved over the years, downtown consists of five distinct districts. The central core—running along the Nicollet Mall, Marquette Avenue, and streets to the east—includes virtually all of downtown's skyscrapers as well as its major shopping venue. Along and to the north and west of Hennepin Avenue is the city's historic warehouse district, once home to giant wholesale firms but now comprising a gentrified mix of theaters, bars, restaurants, and loft-style apartments and offices. The central riverfront, which saw explosive development during the great real estate boom that came crashing to an end in 2008, extends down to the old milling complex around St. Anthony Falls and features much new upscale housing as well as cultural institutions like the Mill City Museum and the Guthrie Theater. The Elliot Park neighborhood on the southeastern side of downtown is a classic mixed-use area. So, too, is the Loring Park neighborhood, which has an especially diverse array of buildings.

Much of downtown Minneapolis is the product of modern-era (post–World War II) development; only in the warehouse district will you find entire blocks still populated by historic buildings. The oldest portion of downtown, the so-called Gateway area along Hennepin and Nicollet avenues near the Mississippi River, was swept away by the hard, unsparing brush of urban renewal in the 1950s and 1960s. This early commercial center formed in the 1850s, as did the huge complex of mills a few blocks to the south at St. Anthony Falls. The completion in 1855 of the first Hennepin Avenue Suspension Bridge, which linked Minneapolis to the slightly older village of St. Anthony on the east side of the river, helped spur growth. The area near the new span became known as Bridge Square, and by the 1870s it was already lined with small brick and stone buildings, including the first Minneapolis City Hall (1873, gone).

From this starting point, downtown gradually spread back from the river like an irresistible tide, reaching something close to its present dimensions by about 1920. Along the way, most of its first generation of buildings disappeared, a trend that was to continue through the twentieth century. Today, little remains from the early age of downtown development. The destruction of the Gateway area, including such monuments as the Northwestern Guaranty Loan (Metropolitan) Building (1890), is the best-known episode of urban renewal gone amok in downtown Minneapolis. Over the years, however, scores of other historic buildings fell one by one—to fire, to old age, or simply to make way for something bigger and newer. As a result, downtown's stock of nineteenth-century buildings is quite small.

Much of what survives, however, is choice, beginning with the magnificent Minneapolis City Hall (started in 1889 but not completed until 1906). Other Victorian-era monuments include such early high-rise buildings as the Lumber Exchange (1886 and later) and the Masonic Temple (1888–90), warehouses like the Langford-Newell Block (1887), churches such as First Baptist (1886) and Wesley United Methodist (1891), and even a few mansions, among them the Alden Smith House (1888) near Loring Park.

During the early decades of the twentieth century, downtown continued to grow both outward and upward, often in spurts reflecting the general state of the American economy. One wave of development began early in the century and culminated in the 16-story First National Bank–Soo Line Building (1914), the city's tallest skyscraper to that point. The so-called City Beautiful movement also flourished at this time, and all manner of schemes were proposed for remaking downtown (and other parts of Minneapolis) on a grand scale. Most of these plans turned out to be no more than grandiose reveries, but one did bear fruit: Gateway Park and Pavilion (1915, gone), which was in many ways the first urban renewal project in the city's history.

Another big burst of development came in the 1920s, when art deco–style skyscrapers reached new heights. The Foshay Tower (1929) remains the best known and most beloved of these Jazz Age monuments, but the Rand Tower (1929) is equally good. The art deco skyscraper era in Minneapolis was brief, however, and ended in 1932 with the completion of the Qwest (Northwestern Bell Telephone) Building.

At the end of World War II, downtown still looked much as it had in the 1920s. Trolleys crisscrossed the streets, shoppers crowded into Nicollet Avenue's four big department stores, and numerous theater marquees illuminated the night along Hennepin. By the early 1950s, however, downtown showed signs of serious decline as half the city, or so it seemed, began moving away to the suburbs. Civic leaders believed that downtown needed to be modernized or risk losing its place at the center of urban life. What followed was a period of astonishing change.

The Gateway project, which got under way in the 1950s, was only the beginning. Over the next two decades, several other seminal developments helped reshape downtown. One was the establishment of the skyway system, which debuted in 1962 with a single glass-and-steel bridge across Marquette Avenue. Five years later, the Nicollet Mall opened, providing downtown with a parklike spine that was also carefully designed to serve the needs of transportation and commerce. A third key development was the IDS Tower. Completed in 1973, the tower not only provided a dominating new presence on the skyline but also set a high standard for design. Since then, 20 or so other skyscrapers—many designed by "starchitects" with international reputations—have grown up around it. The 1970s also saw large-scale redevelopment of the Loring Park neighborhood, including creation of the Loring Greenway (1976).

In the 1980s, city leaders began to look to downtown's past for inspiration. Two historic areas—the warehouse district and the riverfront—became the focus of redevelopment. The transformation of the riverfront, once a derelict industrial landscape, has been especially spectacular. Here, the defining moment may well have been the 1994 reopening (for pedestrians and bicyclists) of the Stone Arch Bridge, a monument from 1883 that now serves as the riverfront's visual and symbolic centerpiece. Parks, museums, restaurants, the new Guthrie Theater (2006), and scores of upscale apartments and condominiums have blossomed in recent years along the riverfront, turning it into one of the city's trendiest precincts.

The once white-hot downtown real estate market began to cool in 2006, and by 2009 the chill was deep and daunting. But there will be other boom times to come down the road, and overall Minneapolis has done remarkably well in creating and sustaining the kind of vibrant downtown that many other American cities of its size can only dream of.

1 The Central Core

The Central Core

The gridiron of streets forming the heart of downtown Minneapolis was laid out in 1854 by surveyor Charles Christmas on behalf of John Stevens, one of the city's first permanent residents (and the builder of a house that still stands, after several moves, in Minnehaha Park). There's nothing unusual about the plat, which like those of many other American downtowns is aligned in relation to a major geographical feature—in this case, the Mississippi River. Years later, Stevens wrote that the streets should have followed the cardinal points of the compass, but the angled downtown grid is actually a good thing, creating a dynamic twist in what is otherwise a very foursquare city.

Stevens made another crucial decision when he established a standard street width of 80 feet, 20 feet wider than in neighboring St. Paul. Although he subsequently regretted this choice as well (narrower streets, he said, would have saved on "the great cost of paving"), it's hard to argue with the result. One reason Minneapolis's downtown grid has remained largely intact over the years is that streets did not have to be widened or moved to accommodate increasing traffic. Unfortunately, Stevens failed to set aside any land for public use along his broad streets, and so Minneapolis has nothing comparable to the downtown squares in St. Paul and many other American cities.

Although Stevens's plat survives, many of his original street names have not. Marquette Avenue, for example, was called Minnetonka, while Third Avenue South was Oregon. Portland Avenue, which ends at St. Anthony Falls, was—appropriately enough—known as Cataract. Most of Stevens's named streets were assigned numbers in the standard Minneapolis manner after the city merged with St. Anthony in 1872.

In the early years of the city, the central business core was between Washington Avenue and the river in what is now called the Gateway District. Houses (including many early Victorian mansions), churches, and institutional buildings gradually filled in the area to the south from Fourth Street all the way to Ninth and Tenth streets. By the late 1870s, however, as the city began its most spectacular period of growth, the business core was already creeping south, swallowing up homes and churches along the way. In 1902, when George Draper Dayton built his department store at Seventh Street and Nicollet Avenue, the intersection became downtown's "100 percent corner"—a status it still enjoys.

Despite a lack of anything like professional city planning, the central core by the 1920s had organized itself into three distinct corridors. Theaters and other entertainment venues clustered along Hennepin Avenue. Retailing, including four major department stores, was the focus of Nicollet Avenue. Marquette Avenue was home to many banks and other financial institutions. This three-pronged arrangement is still in evidence today, though not quite as strongly as it once was.

The Nicollet Mall, created in 1967, is the most significant modern-era intervention in the downtown core (though it could be argued that the skyway system, which dates to 1962, has had an even greater impact). The mall functions as a linear park as well as a pedestrian path and busway, and it is downtown's signature public amenity.

Because of its dynamic history of development, the central core has only a dozen or so buildings constructed before 1900. There are, however, many fine art deco and modern-era buildings scattered throughout the core. These include the wonderfully peculiar ING building (1965), Marquette Plaza (formerly the Federal Reserve Bank, built in 1972), Minneapolis Central Library (2006), the supremely elegant IDS Tower (1973), and two first-class art deco skyscrapers from 1929, the obelisk-shaped Foshay Tower and the Rand Tower.

The Nicollet Mall and Back

Nicollet Mall

1 Nicollet Mall !

Washington Ave. South to
Grant St.

*Lawrence Halprin and Associates
(San Francisco) with Barton-
Aschman Associates (transportation consultants), 1967 /
expanded, 1982 / rebuilt, BRW
Architects, 1990 / Art: sculptures,
fountains, bus shelters, benches,
planters, and other works by
many different artists*

Downtown pedestrian malls were
once the height of fashion, widely
viewed by urban planners as a
way to counteract urban decay
and bring back shoppers fleeing
to the green pastures—and con-
venient parking lots—of subur-
bia. Kalamazoo, MI, inaugurated
the mall era in 1959, and over the
next 25 or so years at least 200
American cities large and small
built downtown malls of one
kind or another. Most turned out
to be failures. The Nicollet Mall,
by contrast, has endured, so much
so that downtown Minneapolis
would be almost unthinkable
without it. The mall's success is
due in part to its being the first
to include a transitway for buses
and taxis. Even now, not everyone
likes this dual arrangement, but
it's doubtful that a pedestrian-
only mall would have worked
over a length of 12 blocks (the
mall was originally eight blocks
long but was expanded four
blocks to the south in 1982).

Nicollet Avenue was a natural
choice for a mall because it had
been Minneapolis's prime shopping street since at least the 1880s.
By the 1950s, however, Nicollet
was losing shoppers to the suburbs, and it was during this anx-
ious period that planning for the
mall got under way. In 1958 the
city brought in Barton-Aschman
Associates to study transportation needs on Nicollet. Four years
later, landscape architect Lawrence
Halprin came on board to design
the mall. The design's visual signature was a sinuous transitway,
which Halprin likened at various
times to a medieval street and an
"urban dance." Halprin rounded
out his design with a lively mix of
fountains, benches, streetlights,
and bus shelters. Works by such
leading sculptors as Alexander
Calder added to the mall's pleasing ambience when it opened
in 1967.

After two decades of hard use,
however, the older portions of
the mall began to look a bit tacky,
even though Mary Tyler Moore's
famous hat toss had by then made
it something of an international
architectural celebrity. In 1990,
with only a few murmurs of pro-
test from preservationists, the
mall was rebuilt with a new
palette of materials, new street
furniture, new artwork, and new
plantings (including Austrian pines
that proved no match for Minnesota winters). The transitway's

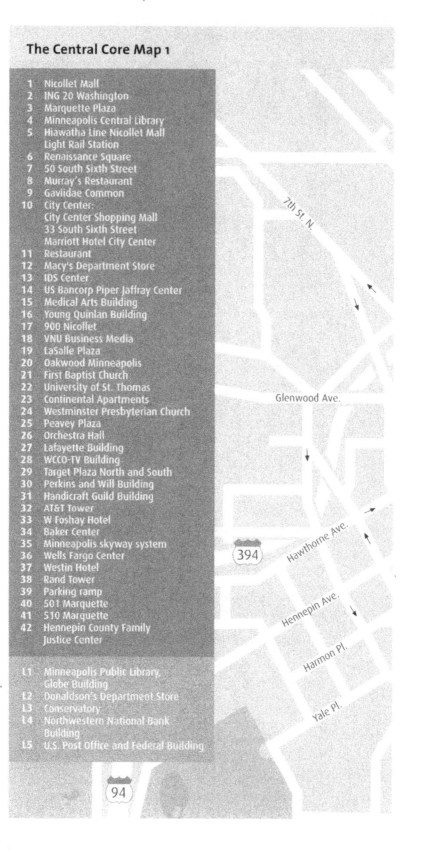

The Central Core Map 1

1 Nicollet Mall
2 ING 20 Washington
3 Marquette Plaza
4 Minneapolis Central Library
5 Hiawatha Line Nicollet Mall
   Light Rail Station
6 Renaissance Square
7 50 South Sixth Street
8 Murray's Restaurant
9 Gaviidae Common
10 City Center:
   City Center Shopping Mall
   33 South Sixth Street
   Marriott Hotel City Center
11 Restaurant
12 Macy's Department Store
13 IDS Center
14 US Bancorp Piper Jaffray Center
15 Medical Arts Building
16 Young Quinlan Building
17 900 Nicollet
18 VNU Business Media
19 LaSalle Plaza
20 Oakwood Minneapolis
21 First Baptist Church
22 University of St. Thomas
23 Continental Apartments
24 Westminster Presbyterian Church
25 Peavey Plaza
26 Orchestra Hall
27 Lafayette Building
28 WCCO-TV Building
29 Target Plaza North and South
30 Perkins and Will Building
31 Handicraft Guild Building
32 AT&T Tower
33 W Foshay Hotel
34 Baker Center
35 Minneapolis skyway system
36 Wells Fargo Center
37 Westin Hotel
38 Rand Tower
39 Parking ramp
40 501 Marquette
41 510 Marquette
42 Hennepin County Family
   Justice Center

L1 Minneapolis Public Library,
   Globe Building
L2 Donaldson's Department Store
L3 Conservatory
L4 Northwestern National Bank
   Building
L5 U.S. Post Office and Federal Building

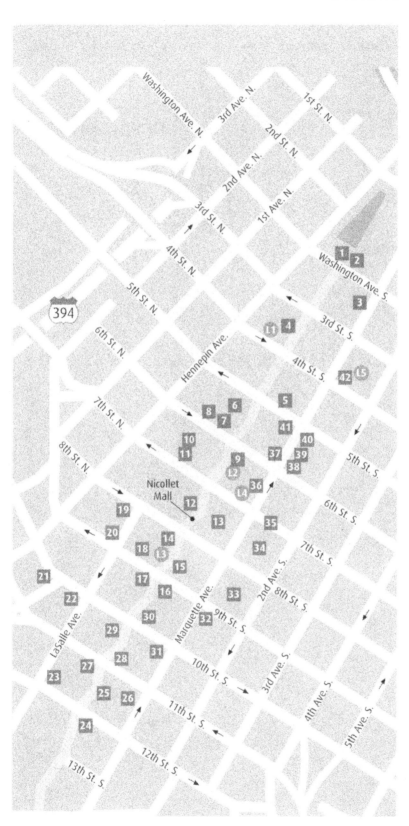

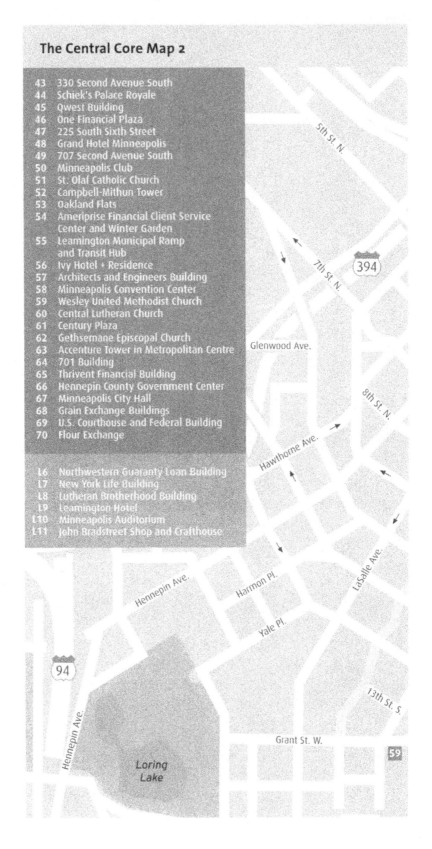

The Central Core Map 2

43   330 Second Avenue South
44   Schiek's Palace Royale
45   Qwest Building
46   One Financial Plaza
47   225 South Sixth Street
48   Grand Hotel Minneapolis
49   707 Second Avenue South
50   Minneapolis Club
51   St. Olaf Catholic Church
52   Campbell-Mithun Tower
53   Oakland Flats
54   Ameriprise Financial Client Service
     Center and Winter Garden
55   Leamington Municipal Ramp
     and Transit Hub
56   Ivy Hotel + Residence
57   Architects and Engineers Building
58   Minneapolis Convention Center
59   Wesley United Methodist Church
60   Central Lutheran Church
61   Century Plaza
62   Gethsemane Episcopal Church
63   Accenture Tower in Metropolitan Centre
64   701 Building
65   Thrivent Financial Building
66   Hennepin County Government Center
67   Minneapolis City Hall
68   Grain Exchange Buildings
69   U.S. Courthouse and Federal Building
70   Flour Exchange

L6   Northwestern Guaranty Loan Building
L7   New York Life Building
L8   Lutheran Brotherhood Building
L9   Leamington Hotel
L10 Minneapolis Auditorium
L11 John Bradstreet Shop and Crafthouse

curvature was also reduced. Halprin groused that the city had "trashed" his original design. Some might argue with that wording, but there's no doubt that Halprin's mall, a child of the 1960s—free-spirited and fun—is gone forever. By contrast, the new mall brings to mind an elderly hippie who's finally been forced to don a suit and get a real job. Be that as it may, the mall remains the long stick of glue that holds downtown together.

2 ING 20 Washington (Northwestern National Life Insurance Co.) !

20 Washington Ave. South

Minoru Yamasaki and Associates, 1965 / Art: Sunlit Straw *(metal sculpture), Henry Bertoia, in lobby*

A temple to the gods of underwriting, built by an insurance company and mixing luxuriousness and high camp in a way that, say, Liberace would have fully appreciated. Along with Ralph Rapson's now demolished Guthrie Theater (1963), it ranks as one of the high points of 1960s modern architecture in Minneapolis. Dubbed by an anonymous wag as the "Japanese Parthenon," the building boasts an attenuated, 85-foot-high portico that visually terminates the Nicollet Mall. The overall fit and finish of the building—faced in white and black marble and placed behind a series of reflecting pools—is also exceptionally high.

Japanese-born architect Minoru Yamasaki is most remembered today as the designer of the destroyed World Trade Center towers in New York City. However, ING 20 Washington is more typical of his work from the 1960s, when he was among a number of leading American architects who produced buildings in a highly formal, classically inspired modernist style.

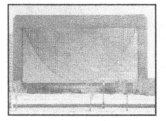

Marquette Plaza

3 Marquette Plaza (Federal Reserve Bank) !

250 Marquette Ave.

Gunnar Birkerts and Associates (Bloomfield Hills, MI), 1972 / renovations and addition, Walsh Bishop Associates, 2002

A hunk of heroic modernism that is now both more and less than it used to be. Built for the Minneapolis Federal Reserve Bank, it employed a novel structural system, with long floors supported by steel catenary arches suspended from towers at either end. This setup allowed the building to span a large plaza below, much like a suspension bridge. The design made structural sense

ING 20 Washington

Minneapolis Central Library

because it minimized the number of columns that would penetrate into what was actually the largest portion of the building—a system of underground vaults and secure work spaces.

Birkerts's inventive design didn't wear well over time. The curtain walls leaked, and the narrow office floors proved inefficient, while extensive use of asbestos fireproofing raised health concerns. In 1997 the Federal Reserve moved out, and it looked for awhile as if the building might be demolished. Instead, a developer bought it and spent $65 million renovating and expanding it for office use. The project included replacing the curtain walls and constructing an 11-story addition to create a larger floorplate. This work was nicely done, but Marquette Plaza in its new configuration has lost a fair share of its original swagger. Still, it's a better outcome than not having the building at all.

4 Minneapolis Central Library !

300 Nicollet Mall

Cesar Pelli and Associates (New Haven, CT) with Architectural Alliance, 2006

When Cesar Pelli was selected over several competitors to design this new library, not everyone was pleased. Pelli is not an especially edgy designer, and at a time when new libraries have often taken on highly unconventional forms (Rem Koolhaas's much-publicized Seattle library being

the prime example), Pelli's proposal seemed conservative.

As it turned out, there was no need to worry. While the library might not satisfy the *avant garde* crowd, it's a luminous building that seems to have instantly endeared itself to Minneapolitans. It's easy to understand why. Suave and gracious, the library delivers that most precious of architectural gifts—natural daylight. Warm, buttery light pours into every corner through bands of fritted glass windows. The result is a building that conveys a sense of clarity and openness perfectly in keeping with the idea of what a public library should be.

On the outside, the building is quite straightforward. Its floors—five on one side and four on the other—are stacked like luminous glass trays, separated by narrow bands of Mankato-Kasota stone. The fritted glass windows, a postmodern touch, depict four common Minnesota scenes: water, evergreens, birch trees, and prairie grass. The library does go for one spectacular gesture in the form of a giant wing that takes flight atop the roof and thrusts out over Nicollet Mall. This aggressive protuberance seems too flamboyant for such an otherwise decorous building, but it does indeed catch the eye.

Inside, the library is organized around a wedge-shaped atrium that functions as a kind of hinge as the building turns slightly to follow the converging lines of Hennepin Ave. and the Nicollet Mall. The bright, welcoming atrium sets the tone for the entire building. It's also impeccably detailed: you see quality in everything from structural connectors to railings to stairway treads.

The library's loft-style floors, which have no bearing walls, were designed for maximum flexibility, since no one knows for sure what the next big thing in information technology may be. Despite its openness, the library has several well-defined interior spaces, including a marvelous children's library with abstract tree forms and a room set aside for teenage readers that features a serpentine bookcase. Plans also call for the addition of a planetarium, thereby restoring a much-beloved feature of the 1960s-vintage library that once occupied this site.

Globe Building, 1895

LOST 1 *Lost buildings of note on this site include the previous* **Public Library** *(1961–ca. 2002, razed) and the romantic* **Globe Building** *(1889–1959, razed), an early skyscraper by Milwaukee architect E. Townsend Mix, who also designed the Metropolitan Building that once stood just three blocks away.*

5 Hiawatha Line Nicollet Mall Light Rail Station

Nicollet Mall at Fifth St.

ESG Architects (with Thomas Rose and Janet Zweig, artists), 2004

The zippiest of all the stations built for the Hiawatha Light Rail Line, with a "rollercoaster" roof and other lively details.

6 Renaissance Square (Andrus Building)

512 Nicollet Mall

Long and Long, 1898 / remodeled, Miller, Hanson, Westerbeck and Bell, 1983

The mall's old-timer, given a showy—if not historically correct—remodeling of the kind common in the 1980s. The second-floor arches aren't original.

50 South Sixth Street

7 50 South Sixth Street

50 Sixth St. South

SOM (Peter Van Vechten), 2001

More ornate than most of the recent skyscrapers in downtown Minneapolis, this 29-story granite and glass office tower features decorative bands of circles in the spandrels between the windows. These shapes are echoed by a polygonal glass entry set—a bit awkwardly—into the corner of the building.

8 Murray's Restaurant

26 Sixth St. South

ca. 1880s (original building) / remodeled, 1946, 1954, 1984 (Paul Pink and Associates)

Garrison Keillor has sung the praises of this downtown institution, and artist Bill Griffith drew it for his *Zippy the Pinhead* comic strip. The restaurant opened in 1946 and since then has offered the luscious promise of a "silver butter knife steak" behind a late

Murray's Restaurant

Moderne facade that, like the restaurant's signature dish, is well aged.

9 Gaviidae Common

651 Nicollet Mall

portion between Sixth and Seventh Sts., Cesar Pelli and Associates (New Haven, CT), 1989 / portion between Fifth and Sixth Sts., Lohan Associates (Chicago), 1991

Taking its name from the Latin term for Minnesota's state bird, the loon, this upscale mall was

Gaviidae Common mall

built in two sections by different architects, and it's a decidedly schizoid affair, at least inside. The two sides are connected across Sixth St. by downtown's only double skyway, one at the second story and the other at the fourth.

The older portion, designed by Cesar Pelli, features a four-story, skylit mall modeled on the airy glass-and-iron arcades of the late nineteenth and early twentieth centuries. It's serenely elegant, almost too much so for the frenetic business of getting and spending. The mall's newer portion, across Sixth St., was designed by Lohan Associates, and its gaudy interior can only be described as the id to Pelli's superego. The, um, high point of the design is a fourth-floor food court that looks to be on loan from a traveling carnival.

LOST 2 *The portion of Gaviidae Common between Sixth and Seventh Sts. was long home to* **Donaldson's Department Store** *(1883 and later). The vacant store was destroyed by fire on Thanksgiving Day 1982.*

10 City Center

Block bounded by Nicollet Mall, Hennepin Ave., and Sixth and Seventh Sts. South

SOM, 1983

City Center Shopping Mall, Nicollet Mall and Seventh St.

33 South Sixth Street (office tower), 33 Sixth St. South

Marriott Hotel City Center, 30 Seventh St. South

This big architectural oaf was plunked down on the city's 100 percent corner in 1983 with no apparent regard for the niceties of urban design. It includes a fortresslike mall with lots of blank walls and a 52-story office tower, both clad in precast concrete panels designed, quite successfully, to achieve maximum unattractiveness. The glitzy Marriott Hotel is a bit better, with mirrored glass walls that at least have some semblance of urbanity, a quality woefully lacking in the complex as a whole.

11 Restaurant (Forum Cafeteria interior) i

Off Seventh St. in City Center

George Franklin, Magney and Tusler, 1929 / 1978 (interior dismantled) / 1983 (interior moved)

Buried within City Center is a reconstituted version of a marvelous art deco interior salvaged from the Forum Cafeteria, once located on this block. The Forum, a fantasy in black and gray glass, was a remodeling job, installed in 1929 inside an old movie theater on Seventh St. The interior was dismantled after the Forum closed in 1978 and later reinstalled, with many changes, as part of a new restaurant.

12 Macy's (Dayton's) Department Store

700 Nicollet Mall

Charles S. Sedgwick, 1902 / additions, Larson and McLaren, 1937, 1947, and later

Known for nearly a century as Dayton's, this retail emporium—now Macy's—is a Minneapolis

icon. Three other large department stores once did business nearby on Nicollet, but Dayton's was always considered the most stylish of the lot. Still well patronized, the store sprawls across a

Macy's Department Store

city block and offers 12 floors of merchandise, along with restaurants, an auditorium, and other amenities. Long the flagship of the Dayton's chain, the store consists of buildings from several eras. The oldest section at Seventh and Nicollet is the most ornate, while the newer portions toward Eighth St. are in the Moderne style of the 1930s and 1940s. Inside, of course, there have been innumerable remodelings. A stroll through the store offers a richly layered shopping experience of a sort that has all but disappeared in the age of big-box retailing.

13 IDS Center i

717 Nicollet Mall

Philip Johnson and John Burgee (New York) with Edward Baker, 1973 / renovated (Crystal Court), HGA, 1998

An extraordinary retailing, office, and hotel complex. Far taller and larger than any previous downtown building, IDS Center brought a new level of modern elegance and a new scale to the city, and it has lost none of its luster over the years. Although newer office towers have risen to within a few feet of the IDS, none so far has been able to match the overall

IDS Center

quality of its design or its gracious urban presence. It also ranks among the best works in the oeuvre of Philip Johnson, a master of architectural fashion who careened from style to style over the years but here achieved something true and poetic.

When it opened in 1973, the center's 57-story tower (built for Investors Diversified Services, now part of Ameriprise Financial) soared 300 feet above the Foshay Tower, long the city's tallest building. Given its bulk, the IDS Center could easily have been a rude giant. Instead, Johnson and partner John Burgee, assisted by Minneapolis architect Edward Baker, turned out a very large building that carries itself with a ballerina's grace.

Much of the building's seeming delicacy stems from the way in which its thin metal window frames project slightly from the walls of blue green glass, producing an airy, cagelike effect.

The framework's attenuated proportions (not unlike those in Gothic architecture) are equally important, creating a sense of vertical thrust. The architects also produced a commercially savvy design that yields up to 32 corner offices per floor. They accomplished this feat of prestige enhancement by means of stepbacks (or "zogs," as Johnson called them) at the corners, which call to mind the serrated profile of a raptor's wings.

At the heart of the center, which includes the 282-room Marquette Hotel, is the Crystal Court, so called because of a glass roof that rises in a series of faceted setbacks from a height of three to eight stories. Johnson once called the court "a frolic space," and while it may be a bit too formal for uncontrolled cavorting, it certainly is fun. It's also the crossroads of downtown, with 50,000 people passing through it on a typical weekday. The court

Crystal Court, IDS Center

was remodeled in 1998 with the addition of a fountain, new benches, and 18 black olive trees.

14 US Bancorp Piper Jaffray Center

800 Nicollet Mall

Ellerbe Becket, 2000

A competent if hardly eye-catching 30-story skyscraper. It's part of a three-block project along this side of the mall that began in the late 1990s, replacing a mix of mostly small, older buildings with skyscrapers, a Target store, shops, and restaurants.

*LOST 3 In 1987 a fancy shopping mall and office complex known as the **Conservatory** opened here. But it was a financial bust from the start and was torn down just 11 years later, making it one of the shortest-lived downtown buildings in the history of Minneapolis.*

15 Medical Arts (Yeates) Building

825 Nicollet Mall

Long and Thorshov, 1923 / addition, Long and Thorshov, 1929 / renovated, Shea Architects, 1993

This Gothicized office structure, notable for its creamy terra-cotta facades, was designed to cater to doctors and dentists. An anonymous "censor committee" once reviewed all rental applications, and professionals found wanting

as to morals or finances were rejected. The first portion of the building, along Nicollet, opened in 1923. Four stories were soon

Medical Arts Building

added. In 1929 a 19-story addition was constructed along Ninth St. Although much of the building has been modernized, its vaulted lobby—resplendent with marble, bronze, and terrazzo—remains largely intact.

16 Young Quinlan Building i

901 Nicollet Mall

Frederick Ackerman (New York) with Magney and Tusler, 1926 / renovated and restored, Ellerbe Becket, 1989

In 1894 Elizabeth Quinlan and Fred Young, who'd met as store clerks, opened a shop offering ready-to-wear clothes exclusively for women. After Young's death in 1911, Quinlan assumed command of the highly successful business. By 1924 she'd made plans for a new downtown store that would offer "the austerity and simplicity of the finest Italian art." The result was this exquisite

Young Quinlan Building

Renaissance Revival building designed by New York architect Frederick Ackerman, who'd already produced a home for Quinlan in the Lowry Hill neighborhood. Ackerman sheathed the ground floor in rusticated Mankato-Kasota stone, while stone pilasters and columns frame windows in the brick walls above. Within, the store features a sweeping marble staircase, crystal chandeliers, and decorative metalwork in iron, brass, bronze, and pewter.

Quinlan died in 1947, but her store remained in business until 1985. Handsomely renovated by new owners in 1989, the building now combines retail and office space. One of the building's lovely brass and pewter elevators is the last in the city still operated by an attendant.

17 900 Nicollet (including Target Store and Retek Tower)

900 Nicollet Mall

Ellerbe Becket, 2001

Taking its cue from theme parks and the spectacular deceits of Las Vegas, 900 Nicollet consists of a group of facades intended to mimic a traditional downtown streetscape with a variety of buildings. The complex, which includes downtown's first Target store as well as an office building known as Retek Tower, uses numerous shades of brick and stone, along with terra-cotta accents, to achieve its effects. The message here seems to be that modern architecture has run out of ideas and that the best that can be done along downtown's most famous street is to play a game of pretend.

18 VNU Business Media (Minnesota Theater storefronts)

50 Ninth St. South (at LaSalle Ave.)

Graven and Mayger, 1928 / theater razed, 1959 / remainder of building remodeled, ca. 1960s

This two-story building occupies part of the site of the Minnesota (later Radio City) Theater, a lavish movie palace that opened in 1928. With just over 4,000 seats and a vast lobby, it was the largest movie theater ever built in the

Minnesota Theater, 1929

Twin Cities. Never a financial success, it fell to the wrecker after
standing for only 31 years. Although this building dates to the
1960s, it probably uses the steel
frame of a shop and office structure that fronted the theater
along Ninth St.

19 LaSalle Plaza

800 LaSalle Ave.

Ellerbe Becket, 1991

There's a hint of art deco in the
upper setbacks of this stone- and
glass-clad skyscraper, but the real
architectural theatrics are within,
where you'll find an arcade with
one of the most elaborate interiors of the postmodern era in
the Twin Cities. The highlight is
a copper fountain that burbles
beneath an oculus sporting fiber-
optic stars and neon lights.

20 Oakwood Minneapolis (Central YMCA)

36 Ninth St. South

Long, Lamoreaux and Long, 1919 / renovated, J. Buxell Architecture, 1994

A handsome exercise in Gothic
Revival, built as a YMCA and
designed by the architects who
produced the similarly styled
Medical Arts Building nearby.
The YMCA moved to a new facil-
ity next door in the early 1990s,
after which this building became
an apartment hotel.

21 First Baptist Church

Tenth St. and Harmon Pl.
(1021 Hennepin Ave.)

Kees and Fisk (later Long and Kees), 1886 / addition (Jackson Hall), Long and Thorshov, 1923 / addition, Station 19 Architects, 1983

First Baptist, founded in 1853, is
among the city's oldest congregations. Its first two churches
were wood-frame structures
located in or near the Gateway
District. In 1886 the congregation
completed this double-towered
stone church that blends the
Romanesque and Gothic Revival
styles. The church lost its original

First Baptist Church

steeples in a 1967 windstorm; the
modern metal steeple atop the
taller tower is an unsatisfactory
replacement. Within, there's an
auditorium with radial seating
and a sloping floor. This arrangement is called the Akron plan,
after the Ohio city where it was
developed.

Terrence Murphy Hall, University of St. Thomas

22 University of St. Thomas

1000 LaSalle Ave.

*includes **Terrence Murphy Hall,** Opus Architects, 1992 / **Opus Hall,** Opus Architects, 1999 / **Law School,** Bulfinch Richardson and Abbott (Boston), 2003 / **Schulze Hall,** Opus Architects, 2005 / Art: The Seven Virtues (fresco, Terrence Murphy Hall), Mark Balma, 1994*

Four modern buildings wearing
Gothic Revival drapery. The highlight here is Mark Balma's 1,900-
square-foot ceiling fresco in the
Terrence Murphy Hall lobby. The
fresco, one of the nation's largest,
presents a vision of the seven
virtues, at least some of which

Westminster Presbyterian Church

most college students are probably acquainted with.

23 Continental (Ogden) Apartments  N *L*

66–68 12th St. South (at LaSalle)

Adam Lansing Dorr, 1910

A six-story building originally constructed as an apartment hotel.
Clad in three colors of brick, the
Continental is in a style sometimes
called Second Renaissance Revival.

24 Westminster Presbyterian Church N

83 12th St. South

*Charles S. Sedgwick and Warren
H. Hayes, 1897 / renovation,
Purcell and Elmslie, 1910–12 /
additions, 1937 (Magney and
Tusler), 1952, and later / sanctuary
renovated, 1998*

A twin-towered Gothic Revival
church that forms a big stone
anchor near the south end of the
mall. It's home to a socially active
Protestant congregation founded
in 1857. This church replaced an
earlier one (on the site of the
Macy's store at Seventh and
Nicollet) that burned down in
1895. Despite the church's massive appearance, the sanctuary is
bright and airy, with 1,300 seats
circling beneath a glass dome.
Architects Charles Sedgwick and
Warren Hayes were old hands
at creating sanctuaries of this

type, whereby a square space
was designed to accommodate
amphitheater-style seating.

Although it retains much of its
historic integrity, the church—
built largely of local limestone—
has seen many additions and
remodelings, including a kinder-
garten room renovated by Prairie
Style masters William Purcell and
George Elmslie. In 1904, the front
gable had to be rebuilt because of
damage from a windstorm that
then moved across the river to St.
Paul and knocked down part of
the Smith Avenue High Bridge.
Additions include a parish house
and chapel (1937) as well as an
education wing from the 1950s.

Peavey Plaza

25 Peavey Plaza

Nicollet Mall and 11th St.

*M. Paul Friedberg and Associates,
1975*

A very "architectural" plaza, rather
hard-edged but on the whole
beautifully designed. Though
only an acre in size, the plaza has
something for everyone—pools,

Orchestra Hall

fountains, walkways, grassy nooks shaded by honey locust trees, and all manner of places to sit. The park is also used by the Minnesota Orchestra for a popular series of summer concerts. There's been talk of renovating the plaza as part of a project to upgrade Orchestra Hall, but preservationists are sure to object to any major changes to Friedberg's original design.

26 Orchestra Hall

1111 Nicollet Mall

Hardy Holzman Pfeiffer Associates (New York) with HGA, 1974 / renovated, Hardy Holzman Pfeiffer Associates, 1997 / addition, Leonard Parker Associates, 2002

This building's aggressive modernism brought industrial chic to Minneapolis, and not everybody was happy about it. The lobby's "power plant" style, complete with exposed vents, drew grumbles from patrons expecting the usual symphony hall. The architect's idea was to remove the taint of class and privilege from the symphony-going experience. Whether this populist strategy succeeded remains open to debate, but the building has won acceptance (though its lobby, revamped in 1997 and slated for expansion in 2011, has never seemed as spacious or inviting as it ought to be). The hall itself, home to the Minnesota Orchestra, is impeccable. An oblong brick box, it seats over 2,500 people and is renowned for its rich, lively acoustics (by Cyril Harris), achieved in part with the help of 100 or so sound-deflectors sprinkled across the ceiling like giant sugar cubes.

27 Lafayette Building

1108 Nicollet Mall

Croft and Boerner, 1922

One of the small glories of the mall, this building wears its polychromed terra-cotta ornament like fine jewelry. The style is Renaissance Revival with what appears to be a Spanish-Moorish twist.

28 wcco-tv Building

Nicollet Mall and 11th St. (90 11th St. South)

Hardy Holzman Pfeiffer Associates (New York), 1983 / renovated, Beecher Walker and Associates (Salt Lake City), 2005

Lafayette Building

This building, supposedly designed to resemble a television tower, is clad in copper and gorgeous blocks of Mankato-Kasota stone. Built during the height of the postmodern era when various nods in the direction of historic architectural styles were much in fashion, it certainly impresses by virtue of the quality of its materials. Still, you'd think a television station would have sought a more lively, modern, and technologically sophisticated image than this rather ponderous building conveys.

Target Plaza North and South

29 Target Plaza North and South

1000 Nicollet Mall

Ellerbe Becket, 2002

A pair of office buildings, one 15 stories and the other 33, that serves as headquarters for the Target Corp. and also provides retail space along Nicollet Mall. The tall south tower, in the form of a sculpted slab, features an architectural light show provided by tall glass pipes within the uppermost floors.

30 Perkins and Will (Essex) Building

Nicollet Mall and Tenth St. (84 Tenth St. South)

Ernest Kennedy, 1913 / renovated, Perkins and Will (Chicago), 2001

A gracious example of the Classical Revival style popular in the early twentieth century.

31 Handicraft Guild Building *L*

89 Tenth St. South

William Channing Whitney, 1907 / addition, 1914

This Georgian Revival building was once home to the Minneapolis Handicraft Guild, as a sign over the Tenth St. entrance indicates. Founded by 12 women in 1904, the guild served as the local outpost of the Arts and Crafts movement then sweeping the United States. The building provided studios and workshops for artisans as well as galleries, classrooms, an auditorium, and a store. In 1918 the guild was dissolved when many of its educational programs were merged into a new art department at the University of Minnesota.

32 AT&T Tower

901 Marquette Ave.

Walsh Bishop Associates, 1991

This skyscraper's oddly splayed top has been likened to an artichoke, but aside from this vegetative gesture, it's just another glass-walled box

33 W Foshay Hotel (Foshay Tower) ! N *L*

821 Marquette Ave.

Magney and Tusler (Leon Arnal, chief designer), 1929 / renovated, Setter Leach and Lindstrom and Shea Architects, 1992 / renovated, Munge Leung Design Associates (Toronto), 2008

A giddy bottle of art deco champagne uncorked just in time for what turned out to be the last wild party of the 1920s. Modeled on the Washington Monument, it's the nation's only obelisk-cum-skyscraper and one of the city's most beloved buildings. At 447 feet, the Foshay was for over 40 years the tallest building in the Twin Cities, and its open-air observatory provided a thrilling view to generations of Minneapolis schoolchildren.

The tower was the brainchild of Wilbur Foshay, a utilities financier and stock plunger who eventually went to Leavenworth

W Foshay Hotel

Federal Prison for mail fraud. Yet Foshay was also something of a rebel in Minneapolis's tight business circle. He built his tower using union labor—an unheard-of step in what was then an open-shop city—and proclaimed that the workers "had produced an honest dollar's worth of work for each dollar paid them." A three-day extravaganza marked the opening of the tower in August 1929. John Philip Sousa and his band played a march composed for the occasion, girls dressed as water nymphs cavorted, and dignitaries delivered speeches. Then the stock market crashed. Foshay's fortune went down with it, so quickly that even his check to Sousa bounced.

W Foshay Hotel interior

The tower, clad in Indiana limestone, is more than just an unusual shape: it's also a superior example of art deco architecture. Rising from a broad two-story base lined with storefronts, the Foshay has four identical windows per floor on each side of the tower. Because of the inward slant, however, corner windows are slightly different on every floor, an inconvenience when it comes to ordering drapes. Foshay's name is carved in ten-foot-high letters beneath the observatory, which wraps around a stepped pyramidal roof.

The public corridors on the ground floor feature terrazzo floors with inlays, a painted ceiling displaying sky and cloud motifs, and ornamental metalwork, including images of the tower worked into bronze elevator doors. These hallways originally converged near an open courtyard that was later filled in with a parking ramp.

Wilbur Foshay, whose mahogany paneled office suite still remains on the 28th and 29th floors and is now home to a bar, was pardoned by President Harry Truman in 1947 but never returned to the world of high finance. He died in Minneapolis on August 30, 1957, exactly 28 years after the dedication of his one-of-a-kind tower.

The tower reopened as a luxury hotel in 2008. The new interiors have a dark, polished, swanky feel, with lots of trendy touches that may not wear especially well over time. But interiors come and go, and what's important is that

the Foshay has found a new use that should ensure its presence on the Minneapolis skyline for decades to come.

Baker Block

34 Baker Center

Block bounded by Marquette and Second Aves. South and Seventh and Eighth Sts.

various architects, 1926, 1928, 1968, and later

includes **Baker Block,** 706 Second Ave. South

Larson and McLaren, 1926

A complex of four interconnected office buildings, including three from the 1920s. The gem of the group is the Baker Block, a 12-story building sheathed in Kettle River sandstone but sporting dramatic terra-cotta ornament in a style so elusive it's been labeled everything from Byzantine to Romanesque to Gothic Revival.

Oldest bridge in Minneapolis skyway system

35 Minneapolis skyway system !

various architects, 1962 and later

Minneapolis's downtown skyway system, the largest in the world, consists of 70 bridges and eight miles of corridors linking about 70 blocks. Its impact has been profound: skyways now shape every aspect of downtown life. The first skyway appeared in 1962 when Leslie Park and his partner, architect Edward Baker, built a bridge (gone) from their new Northstar Center to a building across Marquette Ave. A year later they built a second bridge (which still stands) across Seventh St. to Baker Center.

Park and Baker did not originate the idea of elevated pedestrian walkways. Various urban dreamers had long envisioned such walkways as a means of separating pedestrian and vehicular traffic. In Minneapolis, however, traffic separation wasn't the impetus for skyways; instead, the aim was to boost downtown businesses by sheltering workers and shoppers from Minnesota's extreme weather.

As with Park and Baker's early bridges, most Minneapolis skyways are built and maintained by individual property owners. As a result, bridges vary widely in style. A few, such as the four designed in 1973 for the IDS Center, are exceptionally elegant, but most are fairly simple. The second-story corridors that radiate from these bridges also vary in quality and style.

The system's pluses and minuses have long been debated. The skyways have undoubtedly helped the central core remain vibrant, providing an all-weather connection from one end of downtown to the other. Yet they have also sucked life up and away from its traditional place on the street. Because of this, ground-floor retailing has become a dicey proposition in much of downtown. The lack of obvious connections between street level and the skyways is also a problem. What is certain is that the skyways are here to stay, and however fashionable it may be to decry their mournful effect on street life, the fact is, come January, just about everyone who can use them, will.

36 Wells Fargo (Norwest) Center !

90 Seventh St. South

Cesar Pelli and Associates (New Haven, CT), 1989

Along with the IDS Center and 225 South Sixth, this is one of three 50-plus-story skyscrapers that rule the Minneapolis skyline (the IDS Center is the tallest of the trio by a matter of feet). This building has won wide public favor, and its brightly lit summit makes for a spectacular sight after dark. Wells Fargo Center pays homage to one of the greatest of all skyscrapers—the General Electric (RCA) Building at Rockefeller Center in New York City. The slablike form and sculpted setbacks of that art deco masterpiece are echoed here in Mankato-Kasota stone with white marble accents. The result is a very large building that nonetheless manages to maintain a slender, pleasing profile from most

Wells Fargo Center

vantage points. It's also quite urbane at street level. Within, there's a rotunda (at Sixth St.) that's supposed to be an update of the grand bank lobbies of old, but somehow it doesn't impress quite as much as it should.

LOST 4 *Wells Fargo Center occupies the site of the* **Northwestern National Bank Building,** *constructed in 1929 and best known for its rooftop Weatherball. The 14-story building was destroyed, along with Donaldson's Department Store, in a fire on Thanksgiving Day 1982.*

37 Westin Hotel (Farmers and Mechanics Bank)

520 Marquette Ave. (also 88 Sixth St. South)

McEnary and Krafft, 1941 / additions, McEnary and Krafft, 1955, 1961 / renovated, ESG Architects, 2007 / Art: relief sculptures, Warren T. Mosman, 1941

Now a luxury hotel, this building was originally home to the Farmers and Mechanics Savings Bank (founded in 1870), and it's a major monument in the Moderne phase of art deco. Faced in Mankato-Kasota stone, the

Westin Hotel

building is most notable for bold relief sculptures (of a farmer and a mechanic, naturally) framing the main entrance. Their designer, Warren T. Mosman, headed the sculpture department at the Minneapolis Institute of Arts.

Within, a walnut-paneled banking hall (now the hotel's lobby) was designed to impress—

Westin Hotel lobby

but not overawe—the bank's unpretentious clientele. The tall wings that wrap around the old banking hall were built as offices but today house 214 hotel rooms.

38 Rand Tower ! N i

527 Marquette Ave.

Holabird and Root (Chicago), 1929 / renovated and restored, Shea Architects, ca. 2001 / Art: Wings (sculpture in lobby), Oskar J. W. Hansen, 1929

A skyscraper that's strong in profile but dainty in its details. Chicago architects John Holabird and John Wellborn Root, Jr., were art deco masters, as they were to demonstrate conclusively with their St. Paul City Hall–Ramsey County Courthouse (1932).

This 26-story tower displays classic art deco features: emphatic corners, dramatic verticality, setbacks, and exquisite ornament. The tower is particularly fine at street level, where a delicate scrim of metalwork enframes the windows.

The must-see lobby includes a terrazzo floor inlaid with stars and crescents, marble walls, frosted glass, a spiral staircase, and red elevator doors with nickel-plated ornament. Here, too, you'll find *Wings*, a bronze sculpture by Oskar J. W. Hansen. The statue, as well as references to aviation in the building's ornamental

Rand Tower

Rand Tower lobby

program, reflects the man behind the tower, Rufus R. Rand. A member of a prominent Minneapolis business family, Rand served in the Lafayette Flying Corps during World War I and was involved with the aviation industry for much of his life.

Parking ramp, 517 Marquette Ave

39 Parking ramp (Scandinavian Bank Building)

517 Marquette Ave.

Bertrand and Keith, 1895 / rebuilt, Gage and Vanderbilt, 1925

A bit of Egyptian Revival–style exotica now impaled by a skyway and serving no purpose other than to screen a parking ramp. Long live the pharaoh!

40 501 Marquette (Soo Line– First National Bank Building) *L*

501 Marquette Ave. (also 105 Fifth St. South)

Robert W. Gibson (New York), 1914

This 16-story building was for a time the tallest commercial structure downtown. Like most skyscrapers of its era, it follows a tripartite design scheme (echoing that of the classical column)

with a clearly defined base, a long middle section treated repetitively, and ornate upper stories

501 Marquette

beneath a full cornice. It was built as joint headquarters of the First National Bank and the Soo Line Railroad.

41 510 Marquette (First Federal Reserve Bank)

510 Marquette Ave. (also 75 Fifth St. South)

Cass Gilbert, 1922 / addition, Larson and McLaren, 1955 / renovated, Cerny and Associates, 1974–77

You can't tell it now, but this was Cass Gilbert's greatest work in Minneapolis, built for the newly minted Ninth District Federal Reserve Bank. Gilbert designed a low stone vault of a building, bristling with colossal columns and pilasters and offering nary a window in its lower walls. In the 1950s a 10-story addition was built above the original structure.

U.S. Post Office and Federal Building, 1900

After the bank left in 1972, the columns and other classical details were removed during another remodeling.

42 Hennepin County Family Justice Center (U.S. Courthouse)

110 Fourth St. South

Thorshov and Cerny, 1961 / renovated, ca. 2000

Hard as it is to fathom, this ugly filing cabinet of a building was originally a federal courthouse.

LOST 5 *A towered **U.S. Post Office and Federal Building,** designed by the Supervising Architect of the U.S. Treasury, occupied this site from 1889 until it was razed in 1960 to make way for its dreadful modern replacement.*

Skyscraper City

43 330 Second Avenue South

330 Second Ave. South

KKE Architects, 1980

A cookie-cutter modern office structure, notable only because of what used to be on its site.

LOST 6 *The **Northwestern Guaranty Loan (Metropolitan) Building,** at the corner of Second Ave. South and Third St., was Minneapolis's one indisputable masterpiece of Victorian commercial architecture.*

Built in 1890 and designed by E. Townsend Mix, the 12-story building, clad in sandstone and granite, was especially renowned for its magnificent iron and glass atrium. The building was torn down in 1962.

44 Schiek's Palace Royale (Farmers and Mechanics Bank Building) L

115 Fourth St. South

Long and Kees, 1891–93 / enlarged and remodeled, William Kenyon, 1908

The last small Classical Revival–style bank building left downtown. Today, it's home to a topless bar and restaurant. If you

Schiek's Palace Royale

step inside for a view of the, ahem, scenery, you'll discover a beautiful glass dome that originally illuminated a "ladies banking lobby" but is now the scene of activities not everyone would consider ladylike. Incidentally, the only known natural cave beneath downtown Minneapolis was discovered in this vicinity in 1904 and is sometimes called "Schiek's Cave."

45 Qwest (Northwestern Bell Telephone) Building

224 Fifth St. South (425 Second Ave. South)

Hewitt and Brown, 1932

In the 1930s, long before Ma Bell gave birth to a fractious set of babies, the phone monopoly constructed large office and equipment buildings—mostly in the art deco style—in cities across the United States. These buildings were often of very high quality, as is the case with this 26-story skyscraper, clad in Minnesota limestone and granite. Designed in a version of art deco sometimes called Zigzag Moderne, the building features a series of symmetrical setbacks culminating in a square tower now topped, not very attractively, with a crown of modern electronic equipment. Architects Edwin Hewitt and Edwin Brown were among Minneapolis's outstanding early

Northwestern Guaranty Loan Building, 1892

Qwest Building

twentieth-century designers.
Brown died in 1930, and this
building was the firm's largest—
and last—commission.

One Financial Plaza

46 One Financial Plaza
(First National Bank)

120 Sixth St. South

*Holabird Root and Burgee
(Chicago) with Thorshov and
Cerny, 1960 / renovated, SOM,
1981*

The first big post–World War II
skyscraper in Minneapolis, built
for the old First National Bank.
With its metal-and-glass skin,
this 28-story building brought a
sense of modernity to a skyline

that in 1960 was still dominated
by towers from the 1920s and
1930s. Its basic form—a vertical
slab mounted atop a long, low
base—was widely used for skyscrapers of the time, while its
minimalist detailing reflects the
influence of Chicago architect
Ludwig Mies van der Rohe. The
building's straightforward,
clearly articulated design (essen-
tially classical in spirit) has held
up well.

New York Life Building, 1911

LOST 7 *A fine nineteenth-century
office structure, the* **New York Life
Building** *once occupied this site.
It opened in 1890 and included a
magnificent lobby with two spiral
staircases. The building was razed
in 1958.*

47 225 South Sixth Street
(First Bank Place)

225 Sixth St. South

*Pei Cobb Freed and Partners (New
York), 1992*

The newest of the three 50-plus-
story skyscrapers that hold sway
over the city's skyline. Designed
by James Ingo Freed, it rises from
an L-shaped site in a variety of
cylindrical and rectilinear forms,
culminating in an illuminated
crown that shines over the city
like a halo. A mix of gridded and
horizontal cladding adds to the
complexity of the building, which
includes an 18-story section in
addition to the main 56-story
tower. Lacking vertical momen-

tum, the building isn't nearly as graceful as its two skyline competitors—the IDS Center and Wells Fargo Center.

Within, a winter garden provides some green solace during Minnesota's longest season. As

225 South Sixth Street

originally designed, however, many of the building's public spaces were surprisingly somber, perhaps reflecting the fact that Freed was also working at the time on the Holocaust Museum in Washington, DC.

Grand Hotel Minneapolis

48 Grand Hotel Minneapolis (Minneapolis Athletic Club)

615 Second Ave. South

Bertrand and Chamberlin, 1915 / renovated, HGA, 1992

An old downtown athletic club that has taken on a second life as a ritzy hotel. It's one of half a dozen or so early twentieth-century buildings of virtually identical height (12 stories) that stand along or near Second Ave. South. This uniformity is the result of height limits imposed by the city until about 1920.

707 Second Avenue South

49 707 Second Avenue South (Ameriprise Financial Center)

707 Second Ave. South

HKS Architects (Dallas), 2000

A 31-story skyscraper with cellular, stone-clad facades that project from a curving background of glass.

Lutheran Brotherhood Building, 1955

LOST 8 *An early modernist gem, the **Lutheran Brotherhood Building** opened on this site in 1955. Designed by Perkins and Will of Chicago, it was the first glass-walled office building downtown and was notable for its dainty elegance. It was razed in 1997.*

Minneapolis Club

50 Minneapolis Club

729 Second Ave. South

Gordon, Tracy and Swartwout (New York) with William Channing Whitney, 1908 / addition, Hewitt and Brown, 1911 / addition, Setter Leach and Lindstrom, 2002

The Minneapolis Club was founded in 1883 by members of the city's business, professional, and social elite. The club was at several other locations before constructing this building in 1908. With its clubby English feel, it is precisely the kind of building that new money orders up when it wishes to appear old. The brick building has aged gracefully, abetted by a luxuriant growth of ivy.

51 St. Olaf Catholic Church

215 Eighth St. South

*Thorshov and Cerny, 1955 / addition (including **Chapel of Saints John and Paul**), Bentz, Thompson and Associates, 1980 / addition (parish center), Opus Corporation, 1990 / renovated, HGA, 2000*

Founded in 1940, St. Olaf parish initially occupied a former Protestant church here. After that building was destroyed by fire in February 1953, the parish built this modernistic church. Faced in Mankato-Kasota stone, the church is in the form of an elongated hexagon, with high windows illuminating the nave. There's also a tower containing nine bells salvaged from the old

St. Olaf Catholic Church

church. An addition from 1980 includes an exquisite barrel-vaulted chapel designed by Milo Thompson. A parish center was added in 1990.

52 Campbell-Mithun (Piper Jaffray) Tower

222 Ninth St. South

HGA, 1985

A big glass box with a funny top, which sums up a lot of skyscrapers from the 1980s.

53 Oakland Flats

213–15 Ninth St. South

Harry Jones, 1889

Two round windows set within an ornate panel above the entrance add a lively, if somewhat peculiar, note to this brick and

Oakland Flats

brownstone apartment, which has looked a bit forlorn in recent years.

54 Ameriprise Financial Client Service Center and Winter Garden

901 Third Ave. South

HKS Architects (Dallas) and Maya Lin, 2002

A surprisingly elegant corporate back office building that includes a Winter Garden designed by Maya Lin. Occupying a glassy enclosure set in front of the main mass of the building, the garden is Lin's only work in the Twin Cities, and it has some of the quietly affecting qualities of her most famous design—the Vietnam Veterans Memorial in Washing-

ton, DC. The garden makes especially imaginative use of water, which flows down a portion of the windows like a moving scrim and even freezes over in winter. Inside there are olive trees and an undulating maple floor that brings to mind Minnesota's rolling glacial hills. Lin, in fact, calls the garden "the character of a hill, under glass."

55 Leamington Municipal Ramp and Transit Hub

220 11th St. South (1001 Second Ave. South)

Ellerbe Becket, 1992

Deconstructivism—a style that aimed to subvert normal architectural expectations by creating what look to be elaborately disordered buildings—never enjoyed much popularity in the Twin Cities. But here's a stab at it in a parking ramp that features lots of weird angles.

Leamington Hotel, 1958

LOST 9 *The ramp is named after the* **Leamington Hotel,** *once one of the largest in the city. It stood here from 1905 until its demolition in 1990.*

Ameriprise Financial Winter Garden

Ivy Hotel + Residence

56 Ivy Hotel + Residence (Ivy Tower) *L*

1115 Second Ave. South

Kimball, Steele and Sandham (Omaha, NE), 1930 / addition, Walsh Bishop Associates, 2007

A skyscraper in miniature that, like a child in a roomful of grown-ups, can be hard to spot, especially now that it's been dwarfed by a banal 25-story addition. Never intended to stand alone, it was supposed to be one of four towers at the corners of a giant new Second Church of Christ Scientist (now located in a newer building elsewhere on this block). Alas, 1929 was an inauspicious year to make grand plans, and this tower was the only part of the church ever completed.

The tower—which once included offices, classrooms, and a reading room—is a suave design that mixes the ziggurat form of art deco with mideastern overtones. Its pebbly concrete walls are also distinctive. Renamed Ivy Tower in the 1980s, the building stood vacant and in jeopardy of demolition for over a decade. In 2007, after a number of reuse proposals had come and gone, an addition including 136 hotel rooms and 92 upscale condominiums was wrapped around the tower, which was then renovated.

57 Architects and Engineers Building N *L*

1200 Second Ave. South

Hewitt and Brown, 1920 / restored, MacDonald and Mack Architects, 1985

An elegant limestone and brick building in the Renaissance Revival style. It was designed as a cooperative that included both private offices and shared spaces for the design professionals who were its chief occupants. The names of great architects such as Christopher Wren, Filippo Brunelleschi, and H. H. Richardson are displayed in gold lettering above the third-floor windows. The building has another unusual touch—an enclosed garden on its south side. Within, there's a vaulted lobby.

58 Minneapolis Convention Center

1301 Second Ave. South

Convention Center Design Group (Leonard Parker Associates, Setter

Architects and Engineers Building

Minneapolis Convention Center

Leach and Lindstrom, LMN Architects, and others), 1991 / addition, Convention Center Design Group, 2002 / Art: Seasons of the City *(mural), Anthony R. Whelihan, 2003*

A convention center that's not the overpowering architectural gorilla such buildings tend to be. Opened in 1991 and enlarged 11 years later, the center's well-defined entry towers, glassy lobbies, and carefully detailed precast concrete cladding give it a welcoming presence. Four of the exhibition halls within are topped by copper-clad domes that provide the center's visual signature. The 2002 addition includes a cleverly designed 3,400-seat auditorium that can be reconfigured into smaller spaces with the help of three turntables. Conservatively styled, the center isn't especially exciting, but it does what it's supposed to do in a pleasant Minnesota sort of way.

LOST 10 *The six square blocks consumed by the convention center were at various times home to numerous buildings, most notably the eclectically styled* **Minneapolis Auditorium,** *which opened in 1927 and was razed in 1988.*

59 Wesley United Methodist (The Recovery) Church ⓘ

101 Grant St. East

Warren H. Hayes, 1891 / restored, MacDonald and Mack Architects, 1988–98

One of the city's finest nineteenth-century churches, built for its oldest Methodist congregation,

founded in 1852. The church, which has undergone extensive renovation since the 1980s, offers a colorful take on the Richardsonian Romanesque style. Its walls are largely built of Sioux quartzite, with softer Lake Superior brownstone used for trim. There's also a good deal of Byzantine-style ornament. The

Wesley United Methodist Church

120-foot corner tower originally had a tall wooden cap, but it was removed after a 1949 windstorm.

The massive exterior yields within to a radiant auditorium that seats over 1,000 people beneath a delicate stained-glass dome. The auditorium opens to an adjacent hall by means of a pair of ingenious doors that operate vertically, the top half retracting into the ceiling and the bottom half dropping into the floor.

In 2007 Wesley joined with Central Park Methodist Church in St. Paul to form the Recovery Church.

60 Central Lutheran Church

333 12th St. South

Sund and Dunham, 1928 / addition (bell tower), Bentz/Thompson/Rietow Architects, 2006

A large Gothic church that had to wait over 75 years for its bell

Central Lutheran Church

tower, which was included in the original design but proved too costly to build when the church was constructed in the 1920s. The new one looks just fine.

61 Century Plaza (Miller Vocational High School)

1111 Third Ave. South

Edward Enger, 1932, 1940 / renovated, ca. 1985 / Ankeny Kell Architects, 2000

A Depression-era school building turned into offices. The windows aren't right, however, and the building lost much of its original character in the conversion.

62 Gethsemane Episcopal Church N L

905 Fourth Ave. South

Edward S. Stebbins, 1884

A church that serves the city's first Episcopal parish, founded in 1856. It's constructed of local limestone in a rural English Gothic style that conveys an aura of quaint charm. A corner tower topped by embattlements, rather than the usual spire, is perhaps the church's most distinctive feature. The interior includes open beams, a richly carved screen between the sanctuary and altar, and a stained-glass window designed by Louis Tiffany that depicts the Garden of Gethsemane. The church complex includes a gym once used by the old Minneapolis Lakers basketball team as a practice court. It's now dedicated to the memory of Malik Sealy, a Minnesota Timberwolves player killed in an auto accident in 2000.

63 Accenture Tower in Metropolitan Centre (Lincoln Centre)

333 Seventh St. South

Kohn Pedersen Fox (New York), 1986

With its oddly placed midblock lobby and unusual shape, this large office tower has always seemed awkward. In fact, the building was designed to have two mirroring towers with a shared lobby between them. The second tower never got off the ground, however, and its site is now a grassy plaza. Still, what's here qualifies as a good example of

Gethsemane Episcopal Church

1980s postmodernism, its design hinting at everything from Beaux-Arts Classicism to art deco. The lobby is especially sumptuous.

LOST 11 *The **John Bradstreet Shop and Crafthouse** occupied part of this site from 1904 to 1919. Regarded as the city's leading decorator, Bradstreet incorporated many Japanese elements in the crafthouse, which was a remodeled and enlarged 1870s mansion. The crafthouse, which at its peak employed over 80 workers, closed five years after Bradstreet's death in an auto accident.*

701 Building

64 701 Building

701 Fourth Ave. South

Murphy-Jahn Associates (Chicago), 1984

German-born Chicago architect Helmut Jahn was one of the *wunderkinds* of the 1980s skyscraper boom, designing bright, hyperactive buildings that usually lie somewhere beyond the confining bounds of good taste. Here, Jahn produced a blue glass octagon with salmon-colored accents, and the result is a building as cheerfully inviting as a big lollipop. Yes, it's probably bad for your architectural taste buds, but that doesn't mean you won't enjoy it.

65 Thrivent Financial (Lutheran Brotherhood) Building

625 Fourth Ave. South

SOM, 1981

Pretty wild stuff for Lutherans. Originally constructed for the Lutheran Brotherhood (which became Thrivent in 2001), this

Thrivent Financial Building

17-story building offers a cascading glass curtain wall that ends in a barrel-vaulted dining room poised like a giant glass Tootsie Roll above Fourth Ave. The effect is undeniably dramatic. The other side of the building—a large blank wall—is undeniably uninteresting.

Hennepin County Government Center

66 Hennepin County Government Center

300 Sixth St. South

John Carl Warnecke Associates with Peterson Clark and Associates, 1977

A vision of government as numbing bureaucracy, this 24-story, granite-clad building consists of two towers—one for county offices and the other for courts—separated by an atrium. The building spans Sixth St. South, producing a darkly uninviting tunnel for pedestrians but leaving room for plazas to either side, including one with a large reflecting pool that faces Minneapolis City Hall.

Inside, the public spaces feel cold and oppressive, and the center as a whole seems designed to convey the might and majesty of county government more than anything else. It doesn't make for a pleasant experience. The original design, with open balconies, also proved to be a suicide magnet, and all the balconies later had to be enclosed with glass.

67 Minneapolis City Hall (Municipal Building) ! N i

350 Fifth St. South

Long and Kees, 1889–1906 / restoration, MacDonald and Mack Architects, 2001, 2004 / Art: Father of Waters (statue in rotunda), Larkin Mead, 1906 / Hubert Humphrey (statue at Fifth St. entrance), Roger M. Brodin, 1989

A thundering granite pile that when it rose block upon mighty block in the 1890s must have seemed like the city's dream of itself—powerful, resourceful, built for the ages. No other civic building in the Twin Cities conveys a comparable sense of mass, and the fact that it was constructed in a treacherous swamp of politics, controversy, and debt only makes it more remarkable. Placed on a site well away from the heart of downtown, the building in its early years stood like a stony giant amid rows of small frame houses that served as reminders of the tiny riverside village Minneapolis had been less than half a century earlier.

Minneapolis City Hall

Minneapolis City Hall, Father of Waters *statue*

Known as the Municipal Building, it was designed for both city and county government (although the building is called Minneapolis City Hall today, it is still home to some county offices). This division, saturated in politics, proved awkward. There was also debate over the building's site, a compromise between downtown and "south side" interests. Financing problems plagued the project as well, the cost ballooning from an early estimate of $1.5 million to a final total of $3.6 million. Even the selection of an architect proved controversial despite a much-publicized design competition that drew over 25 entrants. The local duo of Frederick Long and Frederick Kees finally won the job only after much politicking. Given these issues, it's no surprise that the building took nearly two decades to complete.

It was worth the wait. An outstanding example of the Richardsonian Romanesque style, the building is modeled on Boston architect H. H. Richardson's Allegheny County Courthouse in Pittsburgh (1884–88). The sparsely adorned exterior is built of granite from Ortonville, MN, with some blocks weighing over 20 tons. The design displays many Richardsonian Romanesque features, including deep-set arched entrances, bands of windows grouped under elongated arches, turrets and dormers, and two towers, the largest of which

(on the Fourth St. side) rises to 345 feet, making it the tallest structure in the city until the Foshay Tower opened in 1929. As built, the tower had a crow's-nest lookout from which visitors could obtain a view of the city. The lookout is gone, but the tower's 15-bell carillon and its clock (once said to be the world's largest) remain.

The interior, which originally surrounded an open central courtyard, wasn't substantially completed until 1906. It offered an array of splendid spaces, including courtrooms, the mayor's reception room, and the city council chambers. The building's chief interior spectacle, however, is provided by a rotunda off Fourth St. Here, Larkin Mead's gloriously over-the-top statue of a reclining Father of Waters presides over an ornate space featuring a marble staircase, stained glass, carved stonework (including sculptor Andrew Gewond's delightful grotesques), and superb ironwork by Winslow Brothers of Chicago.

Over the years, the building has undergone many remodelings and modernizations, mostly of less than stellar quality. Among the "improvements" was a gallows erected on the fifth floor in 1898 to hang a convicted murderer named John Moshik (the last person to be executed in Hennepin County). In the 1980s the city and county finally developed a restoration plan. So far, the Fourth and Fifth St. entrances, the city council chambers, and, most recently, the rotunda have been restored. Looking better than it has in quite awhile, the building seems ready to go for another 100 or even 1,000 years, should Minneapolis last that long.

Grain Exchange

68 Grain Exchange (Chamber of Commerce) Buildings ! N i

400 Fourth St. South

*Kees and Colburn, 1902 / **Annex, Long, Lamoreaux and Long,** 1909 / addition (trading room enlarged), Bertrand and Chamberlin, 1919 / **North Building,** Edmund J. Prondzinski, 1928 / addition (top three floors), 1955 / renovated and restored, ca. 1985*

These three buildings were constructed for the Minneapolis Chamber of Commerce, established in 1881. Later renamed the Minneapolis Grain Exchange, the complex was home to as many as 500 commodities traders. The oldest of the trio—a ten-story, brick-clad building at the corner of Fourth St. and Fourth Ave.

South—is one of the city's finest early skyscrapers as well as the first constructed with an all-steel frame. Its heavy corner piers, tawny terra-cotta ornament (which includes many agricultural motifs), and exquisite hardware derive from the work of Louis Sullivan, especially his Guaranty Building (1896) in Buffalo, NY. The heart of the building is a fourth-floor trading room that includes a pit, 32-foot-high ceilings, and a balcony with murals furnished by decorator John Bradstreet. The room remained in use until December 2008, when the exchange went to all-electronic trading. The building also has a beautiful main lobby finished in marble, brass, iron, terra-cotta, and ornamental plaster. One of its most distinctive features is a bank of elevators arranged in a slight curve.

A narrow, 12-story Classical Revival–style annex was added to the east side of the building in 1909, and it's nicely done, with boldly scaled terra-cotta ornament. A third building, completed to the north in 1928, offers little of architectural interest.

69 U.S. Courthouse and Federal Building

300 Fourth St. South

Kohn Pedersen Fox (New York), 1997 / Art: plaza, Martha Schwartz, 1997

This courthouse could have served as an elegant, modernist

Grain Exchange lobby

foil to the weighty presence of the Minneapolis City Hall across Fourth St. Instead, it comes across as blandly corporate. To be sure,

paper, but it's proved to be of little earthly use to the public.

Flour Exchange

70 Flour Exchange N *L*

310 Fourth Ave. South

Long and Kees, 1893 / addition, Kees and Colburn, 1909

Holding down one corner of the block otherwise occupied by the U.S. Courthouse, this brick office building is the earliest surviving example in Minneapolis of the straightforward skyscraper style pioneered by Chicago architects in the 1880s. The first four stories date to 1893. The top seven floors, all but identical to those below, were added in 1909.

U.S. Courthouse and Federal Building

it has some nice features—the courtrooms are well handled, and the lobby is by no means unpleasant—yet the building overall isn't very compelling. Neither is its plaza, designed by artist Martha Schwartz and consisting of a field of grassy lumps representing drumlins, a kind of glacial hill found in Minnesota. As high-concept art, the plaza must have looked peachy on

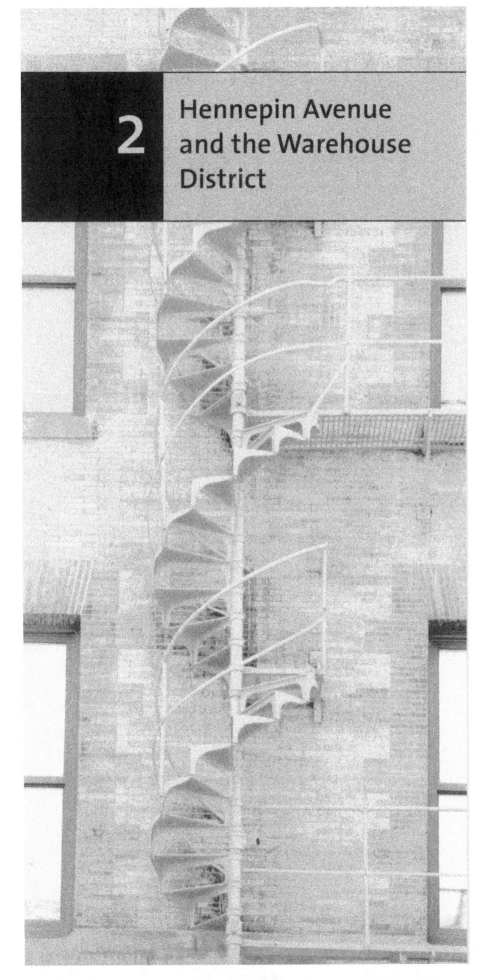

2

Hennepin Avenue and the Warehouse District

Hennepin Avenue and the Warehouse District

Named after Father Louis Hennepin, who "discovered" St. Anthony Falls, Hennepin Avenue is among the city's oldest streets, following a trail that led from the riverbank near Nicollet Island, where the Mississippi could be forded, to Lake Calhoun and points west. The first bridge anywhere across the Mississippi, built in 1855, was at Hennepin, linking Minneapolis to the village of St. Anthony on the east bank of the river.

In its gaudiest days, Hennepin was called the "Broadway of the Northwest." The first large opera house in Minneapolis, the Pence, opened on Hennepin in 1867, and theaters eventually spread down the avenue all the way to Tenth Street. At one time or another, at least 25 theaters operated on Hennepin, which also became home to hotels, the first Minneapolis Public Library (1889, gone), restaurants, bars, arcades, dime museums, and strip joints. Streetcar service made the avenue's attractions readily accessible.

Hennepin's luster faded in the 1960s and 1970s as theaters shut down one by one while porn houses and rough-and-tumble bars flourished. Block E between Sixth and Seventh streets became especially notorious. Its attractions included the legendary Moby Dick's Bar, which generated up to 600 police calls a year—still believed to be a municipal record. The city cleared the block in 1987, and it is now occupied by a truly dreadful hotel-entertainment complex completed in 2003. The reopening of the historic State and Orpheum theaters in the early 1990s, and the Pantages in 2002, was a more positive development. Today much of Hennepin has gone upscale, its old lewd charms largely a memory.

To the north of Hennepin lies the Historic Minneapolis Warehouse District, a gathering of mighty brick buildings that has evolved into one of the city's most desirable places to live, work, and play. Most of the 30-square-block neighborhood now lies within national and local preservation districts, and its trendy transformation would surely astonish the sober businessmen who began building their warehouses and factories here in the 1880s.

Along First and Second Avenues North, development has focused on the renovation of old warehouse buildings for use as offices and housing. Elsewhere in the district, hundreds of new apartments and condominiums have sprung up, many of which proclaim themselves—on thin evidence—to be "lofts." Most of this new architecture is of the inoffensive brick box variety, although edgier buildings like the Bookmen Stacks (2005) embraced a more modern look. When the housing bubble finally burst in 2007, it doused the district's super-hot condominium market, and there's unlikely to be much new construction here for years to come.

Rail lines—the first arrived in 1867—drove development of the warehouse district, which by the 1890s was a bustling mix of sawmills (along the river), saloons (mainly along Washington Avenue), and wholesale and manufacturing firms, including numerous farm implement dealers. The district's sturdy brick buildings—mostly constructed between 1885 and 1920—were designed by some of the city's leading architects. At least one, Harry Jones's Butler Brothers Warehouse (now Butler Square) of 1906, is among the city's architectural masterpieces.

The trade didn't last forever, and as early as the 1930s the fortunes of the warehouse district began to decline. But because its buildings weren't generally in the path of development, they largely escaped the convulsions of urban renewal in the 1950s and 1960s. Instead, they waited like dormant plants for new life. It came in the form of tax credits for historic renovations in the 1970s, along with a deepening public interest in preservation. Artists and entrepreneurs formed the vanguard of this urban renaissance, which despite the bleak economic realities of the moment still qualifies as one of the city's great success stories.

Hennepin Avenue and the Lower Warehouse District

Hennepin Avenue Suspension Bridge

1 Hennepin Avenue Suspension Bridge N L

Across Mississippi River to Nicollet Island

Howard Needles Tammen and Bergendorf (engineers), 1990

This stubby suspension bridge was built in part to "recall" two earlier suspension spans here. But there was no structural rationale for it, since suspension bridges these days are normally used for spans of several thousand feet. This bridge spans only 625 feet, which explains why the towers are so low compared to those of other, far more graceful suspension bridges elsewhere.

POI A First Bridge Park N L

Beneath Hennepin Avenue Bridge at West River Pkwy.

2001

Here you'll find excavated footings of the first three Hennepin Ave. bridges—suspension spans built in 1855 and 1876 and a steel arch bridge completed in 1891 that was replaced by the present bridge. Part of the iron anchoring for the 1876 bridge is on display.

2 Federal Reserve Bank N L

90 Hennepin Ave.

Hellmuth Obata and Kassabaum (Kansas City), 1997

The first two Federal Reserve banks in Minneapolis were muscular buildings that conveyed a sense of power and prestige. This building, by contrast, tries hard not to be monumental. Instead, it offers a wall of curving glass, a dainty clock tower that looks as

Federal Reserve Bank

though it might have come from a 1950s Scandinavian town hall, and a riverfront plaza designed to show that the bank can be a good urban neighbor. Call it the kinder, gentler Federal Reserve, but don't call it a bold, imaginative, or exciting work of architecture.

LOST 1 *For many years this was the site of the* **Great Northern Station,** *which opened in 1914 and replaced an earlier* **Union Depot** *just across Hennepin Ave. The station had a stately, colonnaded facade and was one of the city's prominent monuments. Like many another old train depot, it ended its days as a vacant hulk; it was torn down in 1978.*

Hennepin Avenue and the Warehouse District

1   Hennepin Avenue Suspension Bridge
2   Federal Reserve Bank
3   Lumber Exchange
4   Hiawatha Line Warehouse District/
    Hennepin Avenue Station
5   Minnesota Shubert Performing Arts
    and Education Center
6   Hennepin Center for the Arts
7   Block E
8   Pantages Theater and Stimson
    Building
9   Girard Building
10 State Theater
11 Chambers Hotel
12 Orpheum Theater
13 First Avenue and 7th Street Entry
14 Target Center
15 Gluek Building
16 Butler Square
17 Wyman-Partridge Building
18 Wyman Building
19 300 First Avenue North
20 McKesson Building
21 Fourth Street Ramp, Fifth Street
    Ramp, Seventh Street Ramp

22 Target Field
23 Ford Centre
24 Wells Fargo Branch Bank
25 Bookmen Stacks
26 Traffic Zone Center for Visual Art
27 Washington Avenue
28 Pacific Block
29 Andrews Building
30 Security Warehouse Lofts
31 Tower Lofts
32 HGA Offices
33 Ames and Fischer Building
34 Itasca Lofts
35 Minnesota Opera Center & Gaar
    Scott Historic Lofts
36 River Station
37 Creamette Historic Lofts
38 Heritage Landing
39 Riverwalk Condominiums
40 Ribnick Furs Building
41 Prisma International & Chicago
    House & Foster House
42 Realty Co. Warehouse

Olson Memorial Hwy.

5th St. N.

6th Ave. N.

7th St. N.

Border Ave. N.

3rd Ave. N.

Glenwood Ave.

94

Glenwood Ave.

Hawthorne Ave.

Hennepin Ave.

394

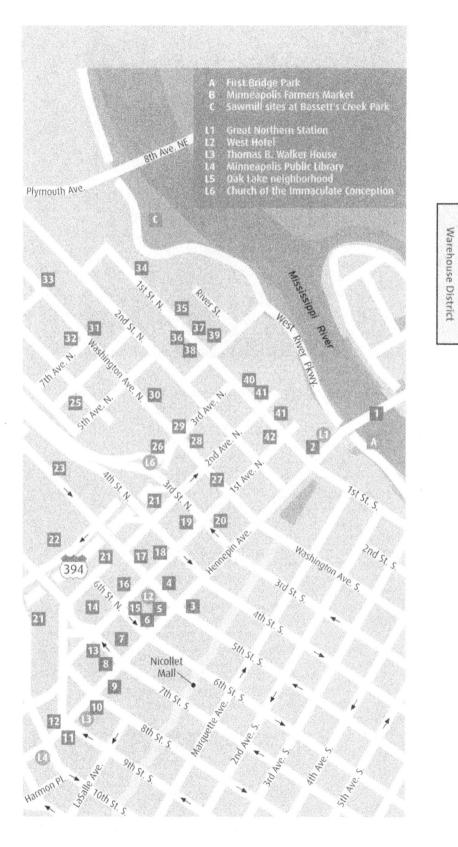

A   First Bridge Park
B   Minneapolis Farmers Market
C   Sawmill sites at Bassett's Creek Park

L1   Great Northern Station
L2   West Hotel
L3   Thomas B. Walker House
L4   Minneapolis Public Library
L5   Oak Lake neighborhood
L6   Church of the Immaculate Conception

Warehouse District

Lumber Exchange

3 Lumber Exchange N L

425 Hennepin Ave.

Long and Kees, 1886, 1891 / addition (top two stories), Harry Jones, ca. 1909 / remodeled, Wheeler Hildebrant, 1980

Downtown's oldest "skyscraper," and the city's tallest when it opened in 1886. Like Long and Kees's contemporaneous Minneapolis City Hall, this building—with its arched entrances and walls of rough-cut granite and sandstone—is in the Richardsonian Romanesque style. Its undulating bay windows and lack of ornament except around the entrances also show the influence of Chicago skyscrapers of the period. The building was enlarged in 1891 along its Hennepin Ave. side. Later, two stories (faced in brick) were added to the top. It was once home to many lumber dealers, but that trade largely vanished with Minnesota's pineries by 1910. A renovation in the 1980s brought back some of the original interiors, including a marble-clad lobby and decorative metalwork.

4 Hiawatha Line Warehouse District/Hennepin Avenue Station

Fifth St. between Hennepin Ave. and First Ave. North

ESG Architects, 2004

The northern terminus of the Hiawatha Line, which opened in 2004, restoring light rail service to Minneapolis exactly 50 years after the last streetcar rattled off to oblivion. The line connects downtown to the Minneapolis–St. Paul International Airport and the Mall of America. The Hiawatha Line's 17 stations, all designed by local architects, vary in style. Some go for a glassy, high-tech modern look, while others drift in the direction of nostalgia. This station seems to fall between those two poles.

5 Minnesota Shubert Performing Arts and Education Center (Sam S. Shubert Theater) N L

516 Hennepin Ave.

William Albert Swasey (New York), 1910 / renovation, Miller Dunwiddie Architects, 2009

A monument to either the wisdom or the folly of historic preservation, depending on your point of view. This playhouse turned movie theater, which had been vacant for nearly 20 years, was moved here in February 1999 at a cost of $4.7 million even as critics questioned whether it was a wise expenditure of public dollars.

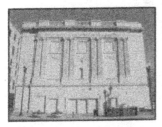

Minnesota Shubert Performing Arts and Education Center

The 1,100-seat theater, downtown's oldest, features a facade of creamy terra-cotta with classically derived ornament. Although hardly a great building, it has historic value as the last theater of its kind in Minneapolis. Architect Albert Swasey specialized in theaters and was known for producing technically sophisticated buildings with excellent sight lines.

The theater—all 5.8 million pounds of it—was moved because it stood in the path of development plans for the so-called Block E. Artspace, a nonprofit developer, bought the building (minus its floor and stage house, which couldn't be moved). The city then paid to move the structure so that it could be renovated into an arts center. However, it took Artspace ten years to raise the $42 million needed to renovate the Shubert into a center for dance, theater, and art. Three dance companies will be based in the theater, which will have just over 500 seats in its new configuration and will be linked by an atrium to the Hennepin Center for the Arts. The Shubert is set to open in 2011.

LOST 2 The **West Hotel,** *the finest in the city when it opened in 1884, once occupied this site. The hotel had over 400 rooms and a huge skylit lobby. It was demolished in 1940.*

6 Hennepin Center for the Arts (Masonic Temple) N *L*

528 Hennepin Ave.

Long and Kees, 1888–90 / renovated, Svedberg-Vermeland Architects, 1979

A fine old Victorian, its craggy walls of Ohio sandstone animated by intricate carvings, quasi-Egyptian columns, projecting bays and balconies, and whatever else the architects could think of to stir up some Masonic excitement. Two Moorish onion domes once capped the composition, but they succumbed to age and rot and were removed. As designed, the

West Hotel, 1900

Hennepin Center for the Arts

temple included retail and office space plus four large Masonic halls stacked one atop the other at the northeast corner. The largest of the halls occupied most of the top floor. The building has been an arts center since 1979.

7 Block E

Hennepin Ave. between Sixth and Seventh Sts.

Antunovich Associates (Chicago), 2002–3 / includes stores, restaurants, bar, and parking; **Graves/ 601 Hotel;** *and* **Crown Theatres 15**

A cartoon of a development that presents architecture as a kind of entertainment for the same masses who crowd into Disney World or roam the Las Vegas strip. It's easy to dislike everything about this complex, from its cheap-looking stucco and precast concrete details to its almost complete divorce of structure from facade, but it's much harder to dismiss the reality of what it represents. Commercial architecture of all kinds is growing ever lighter, showier, and more disposable, and Block E in its own crummy but calculated way perfectly expresses these trends.

8 Pantages (Mann, RKO Pan) Theatre and Stimson Building i

700–710 Hennepin Ave.

Kees and Colburn and B. Marcus Priteca (Seattle), 1916 / renovated, 1926, 1946, 1961 / restored, HGA, 2002

This old vaudeville theater stood vacant for 18 years before the City of Minneapolis stepped in to buy and restore it. Reopened in 2002, it now serves as a venue for touring shows, concerts, and other live performances. When it opened in 1916, it was part of a circuit operated by Alexander Pantages. The theater went through three names and an equal number of remodelings before beginning its long hibernation in 1984.

The 1,000-seat auditorium has lavish plasterwork, a skylight, and a two-level balcony, all designed by B. Marcus Priteca of Seattle in a style sometimes called "Pantages Greek." Today the Pantages is one of three restored theaters that create a distinctive entertainment zone along Hennepin between Seventh and Ninth Sts.

Girard Building

9 Girard (Teener) Building

727–29 Hennepin Ave.

Magney and Tusler, 1922

A sliver of a building faced in terra-cotta and one of the last of its kind downtown. Many of the original downtown lots were only 20 feet wide, leading to clumps of narrow buildings that once formed intriguing, highly varied streetscapes. It's anyone's guess how long this little building will survive.

10 State Theatre i

805 Hennepin Ave.

J. E. O. Pridmore (Chicago), 1921 / restored, Ellerbe Becket with Ray Shepardson, 1991

When it opened on February 5, 1921, this was the largest and most opulent theater yet built in Minneapolis. Thousands turned out for the opening festivities, during which 20 female ushers equipped with swagger sticks kept the crowds in line. Architect J. E. O. Pridmore adorned the State's terra-cotta facades with floral ornament, droopy Ionic column capitals, eagles perched atop pilasters, and even four grinning faces mounted along the cornice. He described the style as "Free Italian Renaissance." Make that very free, and you've probably got it right. Within, the 2,200-seat auditorium features colorful plasterwork (including figures representing Music, Drama, and something called the Muse of Cinema), crystal chandeliers, and murals depicting "bountiful" (i.e., bosomy) nudes.

Though built to accommodate stage and film presentations, the State functioned mainly as a movie theater until it closed in 1975. A church later occupied the building, which was purchased by the city and restored in 1991 as part of the LaSalle Plaza project in the same block.

LOST 3 *The* **Thomas B. Walker House** *occupied this site from 1876*

State Theatre

to about 1920. Walker was a lumber and real estate baron and a great collector of art. A public gallery he established at his house in 1887 evolved into what is now the Walker Art Center.

11 Chambers Hotel (Fairmont Apartment Hotel)

901 Hennepin Ave. (also 9 Ninth St. South)

Adam Lansing Dorr, 1908 / renovated and enlarged, Rockwell Group (New York) with Shea Architects, 2006

An old apartment hotel given an upscale makeover. It's one of many projects that have changed the texture and feel of this part of Hennepin in recent years.

Orpheum Theatre interior

12 Orpheum (Hennepin) Theatre i

910 Hennepin Ave.

Kirchhoff and Rose (Milwaukee), 1921 / renovated, Miller Dunwiddie Architects, 1989 / renovated and restored, HGA, 1993

With 2,650 seats, this former vaudeville house is the largest of the three restored theaters along Hennepin. When it opened on October 16, 1921 (with the Marx Brothers as headliners), it was billed as the "biggest vaudeville theater west of New York."

The theater is actually two separate but connected structures: a long, fingerlike lobby that extends back from a narrow facade along Hennepin and the auditorium itself, which is well to

the rear paralleling Hawthorne Ave. Much remodeled over the years, the restored lobby includes six terra-cotta bas-relief sculptures inspired by the Roman art of Pompeii.

The auditorium is a testament to the colorful art of the plasterer, offering a ripe abundance of garlands, swags, medallions, and other decorative features. There's also a ceiling dome that glitters with 30,000 squares of aluminum leaf. Originally, the theater had a shallow stage, but it was extended by 20 feet as part of the restoration project so that the theater could accommodate large Broadway shows.

Minneapolis Public Library, 1905

LOST 4 *The first* **Minneapolis Public Library,** *a Richardsonian Romanesque building, was built in 1889 at Tenth St. and Hennepin Ave. at what is now the site of a parking lot for First Baptist Church. The library was demolished in 1959.*

13 First Avenue and 7th Street Entry (Greyhound Bus Depot)

701 First Ave. North (29 Seventh St. North)

Lang and Raugland, 1936 / remodeled, ca. 1970

Known for its association with performers like Prince, this nightclub began life as a Greyhound bus depot designed in the Streamline Moderne variant of art deco, with sweeping curves and long bands of windows. After Greyhound left, the building reopened in 1970 as a club. Now painted black with a field of white stars, the old depot retains many original interior features and would be a good candidate for restoration if the music ever dies.

First Avenue and 7th Street Entry

14 Target Center

600 First Ave. North

*KMR Architects and Pfister
Architects, 1990*

It's too big for its site, its facades
have the look of bad wallpaper, it
makes little effort to fit in with its
historic surroundings, its steeply
pitched nosebleed seats will give
you instant vertigo, and it's home
to a consistently mediocre basketball team—the Minnesota Timberwolves. The only good news is
that, given the typical life span of
arenas these days, it probably
won't be around for very long.

Gluek Building

15 Gluek Building *L*

16 Sixth St. North

*Boehme and Cordella, 1903 /
interior rebuilt after fire, 1989 /
Art: mural, Herman Krumpholz*

A terra-cotta facade with baroque
aspirations makes this one of
downtown's liveliest little buildings. There's also a *trompe l'oeil*
mural on one side that depicts a
Venetian scene. The building was
constructed for the Gluek Brew-
ing Co., which was founded in
1855 and operated a brewery in
northeast Minneapolis until 1965.

16 Butler Square (Butler Brothers Warehouse) ! N *L*

100 Sixth St. North

*Harry Jones, 1906 / renovated,
Miller Hanson and Westerbeck
with Arvid Elness, 1976–81 / Art:
Circus Flyers (figures suspended
in atrium), George Sefal, 1981*

One of the city's architectural
masterpieces, a sternly poetic
mass of wine-colored brick that
conveys the commercial might of
Minneapolis at the dawn of the
twentieth century. It's also significant as the first, and still the
finest, warehouse renovation in
the historic district here. The job
wasn't done perfectly—the windows, for example, should have
been set farther back in their
reveals—but it paved the way for
many more renovations to come.

Butler Square atrium

The building was constructed
for Butler Brothers, a wholesaling
firm founded in Boston in 1877.
The firm later established (in
1927) the Ben Franklin chain of
variety stores. Architect Harry
Jones was one of those suave,
versatile designers—Cass Gilbert

Butler Square

was another—who could work successfully at any scale, and here he produced one of his outstanding works. The building combines great power with subtle details: a corbeled (stepped-out) cornice, narrow windows grouped vertically so as to resemble oversized Gothic lancets, twin belt courses that define the base, and deeply inset ground-floor openings that reveal the heft of its masonry walls.

Within, the building was a timber-framed loft structure designed to meet the heavy demands of warehousing. The architects of the renovation that began in 1976 carved an atrium out of the interior and surrounded it with glass-walled offices inserted into the timber framework, all with beautiful results.

17 Wyman-Partridge Building (Wyman Partridge and Co. Factory) N *L*

110 Fifth St. North

Kees and Colburn, 1916

At 12 stories, this brick and terra-cotta building is the tallest in the warehouse district. In 1990 Prince founded a nightclub called Glam Slam on the ground floor, but both it and a successor are now gone.

18 Wyman (Wyman Partridge and Co.) Building N *L*

400 First Ave. North

Long and Kees, 1896 / addition, Kees and Colburn, 1910

Renaissance Revival elements applied to a standard brick warehouse. Bands of terra-cotta ornament and a Doric frieze enliven the ground floor, while five large arches and a massive cornice

Wyman Building

balance off the composition at the top. This building served as the headquarters of Wyman Partridge and Co. Founded in 1874, the company by the early 1900s operated from four buildings in the warehouse district.

19 300 First Avenue North (Langford-Newell Block) N *L*

300 First Ave. North

William H. Dennis, 1887 / renovated, KKE Architects, 1985

An impressive building, notable for stone and brick arches that seem to lift it above the street as though it were mounted on stilts. The building's terra-cotta ornament includes lion heads and a bulging corner cartouche that

300 First Avenue North

displays a train and a clipper ship. Built for businessman Robert Langdon (memorialized by a decorative "L" in the terra-cotta work), the building was once occupied by the wholesale grocery firm of George L. Newell and Co., which later became SuperValu.

20 McKesson Building (Harrison Block, Lyman-Eliel Drug Co.) N L

24 Third St. North

Warren H. Hayes, 1893

A warehouse that mixes Romanesque and Classical elements without doing any insult to either.

21 Fourth Street Ramp, Fifth Street Ramp, Seventh Street Ramp

Second Ave. North between Third and Tenth Sts.

Stageberg Beyer Sachs, 1989 (Fifth St.), 1991 (Seventh St.), 1992 (Fourth St.)

Three city-built parking ramps that—unlike many other post-modern structures with pretensions of being "contextual"—actually do fit into their historic environment.

22 Target Field

Block bounded by Third Ave. North, Fifth and Seventh Sts. North, and railroad tracks

HOK Sport (Kansas City) and HGA, 2010

Opening in 2010, this $544 million, 40,000-seat open-air baseball park for the Minnesota Twins should provide the team's fans with a much more enjoyable experience than did the frumpy old Metrodome. The park's rather tight site isn't perfect (there's an aromatic garbage incinerator across the street), but it's close to mass transit and large public parking ramps, and the field itself offers downtown skyline views from many of the seats.

New major league ballparks have usually opted for either nostalgia (as at Camden Yards in Baltimore) or a high-tech, industrial look (as exemplified by Progressive Field in Cleveland). Target Field is a bit of both. Much of the park is faced in Mankato-Kasota stone to blend in with the warehouse district's masonry buildings, but there are also glass-walled elements around an entry plaza at Third Ave. North and Seventh St. North. For fans, Target Field promises an intimate view of the game, with fewer distant upper-deck seats than any other major league ballpark. Play ball!

Target Field

23 Ford Centre (Ford Assembly Plant) N L

420 Fifth St. North

Kees and Colburn with John Graham (Seattle), 1914

The Ford Motor Co. produced 400 Model T automobiles a day here before moving its operations to the assembly plant that still operates in St. Paul (but is scheduled to close in 2011). Honeywell Corp. later occupied this building, which is now used for offices.

POI B Minneapolis Farmers Market

312 East Lyndale Ave. North

1933 and later

This popular market, located beside an elevated stretch of Interstate 94, lies at the southern edge of what was once a genteel neighborhood of Victorian homes.

LOST 5 *In 1880 brothers Samuel and Harlow Gale platted a 60-acre subdivision here called* **Oak Lake.** *The neighborhood, which had winding streets built around a pond, attracted upper-middle-class homebuyers for a time but soon began to decline. Most of the neighborhood's old houses were cleared away in the 1930s. Today, Oak Lake Ave. serves as the only reminder of this lost part of the city.*

24 Wells Fargo (Northwestern National) Branch Bank

615 Seventh St. North

Ackerberg and Associates, 1969

Grand kitsch from the 1960s, blissfully free from the burden of good taste. With its sloping walls, restless massing, and aura of otherworldly oddness, this two-toned brick wonder would make a fine temple for a religious cult. Alas, the only almighty it serves at present is the dollar.

Bookmen Stacks

25 Bookmen Stacks

345 Sixth Ave. North

James Dayton Design and LSA Design, 2005

Many of the newer buildings in the warehouse district go in for nostalgia of one kind or another. This glass- and zinc-clad building, by contrast, makes no attempt to hide its aggressive, forthright modernism. While the building wouldn't turn many heads in California (where its architect, James Dayton, once worked for the modern master Frank Gehry), it certainly stands out here and plays off nicely against the masonry structures around it.

Wells Fargo Branch Bank

Traffic Zone Center for Visual Art

26 Traffic Zone Center for Visual Art (Moline, Milburn and Stoddard Co.) N *L*

250 Third Ave. North

Joseph Haley, 1886 / addition, 1925 / renovated, 1995

A rugged stone industrial building converted in 1995 to artist studios and offices. It's a strict and economical design for its time, with nary a hint of the ornament so beloved by Victorian architects. The building, which received a seamless three-story addition in 1925, achieves its effects through the massing of its limestone walls, the rhythmic pattern of its windows, and the use of belt courses between the floors. It was built as a factory and showroom for the Moline, Milburn and Stoddard Co., a farm equipment manufacturer.

LOST 6 *The* **Church of the Immaculate Conception,** *predecessor of the Basilica of St. Mary, was built at the corner of Third St. and Third Ave. North in 1872. The Gothic structure was for many years the city's largest Catholic church. However, as warehouses swallowed up much of this neighborhood, church leaders decided to erect a new basilica, which opened in 1914 on a site near Loring Park. The old church was then demolished.*

From Lumber to Lofts

27 Washington Avenue

This long avenue, which connects North Minneapolis to downtown and the University of Minnesota, has a right-of-way of 100 feet, among the widest of any street in the Twin Cities. It was designed as the main avenue in the first plat of Minneapolis made for John Stevens in 1854. Though still an important street, it's not as heavily traveled as it once was because traffic has shifted to Interstate 94.

28 Pacific Block N *L*

218–28 Washington Ave. North

ca. 1865 (possibly later) / renovated, Adsit Architecture and Planning, 2004

This one-time hotel is believed to be the oldest building in the warehouse district.

29 Andrews (Jackson) Building N L

300–312 Washington Ave. North

Ernest Kennedy, 1897 / addition (fifth floor), Ernest Kennedy, 1899

Like Butler Square, this building uses Gothic detailing—most notably the pointed-arch windows on the fourth floor—to dress up what is otherwise a utilitarian structure. The glassy ground floor was built to serve as a storefront, while the upper floors were warehouse space.

30 Security Warehouse Lofts (W. J. Dean Co.) N L

404 Washington Ave. North

Bertrand and Chamberlin, 1902 / renovated, Oertel Architects

A warehouse built in a rather straitlaced classical style, with large brick diamonds providing most of the ornamental punch. Now converted to condominiums, it was built for William J. Dean, a farm implement dealer.

31 Tower Lofts (Northern Bag Co.) N L

700 Washington Ave. North

Hewitt and Brown, 1920 / renovated, ESG Architects, 2005

The tower that gives this building its name is a landmark along this part of Washington Ave. Like so many other large industrial structures from the early 1920s, the building has a Gothic air to it, but there are also hints in the tower's subtle setbacks of the art deco style to come. The building became an artists' cooperative in the 1980s but was later converted to condominiums.

32 HGA Offices (Loose-Wiles Biscuit Co.) N L

701 Washington Ave. North

Hewitt and Brown, 1910 / renovated, HGA and Miller Dunwiddie Architects, 2002

Now home to one of the state's largest architectural firms, this old biscuit factory is an impressive specimen of industrial design. Its style is elusive: the ground floor hints at Renaissance Revival, but the terra-cotta panels pinned to the upper corners like big brooches seem to be in the spirit—if not the exact style—of Chicago architect Louis Sullivan.

33 Ames and Fischer Building (Deere and Webber Co.) N L

800 Washington Ave. North

Kees and Colburn, 1902, 1910 / renovated, 2000, 2005

One of the finest buildings in the warehouse district. The six-story

Tower Lofts

portion went up first, in 1902. The taller section to the north was added in 1910. The building's sloping lower walls, arched entrance, deeply inset windows,

Ames and Fischer Building

curving parapet (on the six-story section), and clean lines are all reminiscent of Chicago warehouses designed by Louis Sullivan. There's even some Sullivanesque ornament around the restored entry. Used today for offices, the building originally served the Deere and Webber Co., a branch of the Illinois-based John Deere Co.

POI C Sawmill sites at Bassett's Creek Park

West River Pkwy. near Eighth Ave. North

The land that forms this park at the mouth of Bassett's Creek is all fill. Much of it was dumped by sawmills—there were at least seven at one time or another—that began clustering along the river here as early as the 1850s. All were gone, as were most of Minnesota's pineries, by 1910. Bassett's Creek, which is diverted into a tunnel through the downtown area, is named after Joel Bassett, a settler from Maine who homesteaded a farm near here in 1852 and later operated the first steam-powered sawmill on the west bank of the river at the foot of Seventh Ave. North.

34 Itasca Lofts (Itasca A and B warehouses) N L

702–8 First St. North

Long and Kees, 1886 / renovated, Cuningham Architects, 1984

Although this yellow brick building looks like one structure, it's a pair of identical warehouses separated by an internal wall. With their broad brick arches, including a pair that recedes into the parapet, the warehouses have a light and fanciful quality that sets them apart from the weightier buildings all around. They were among the first warehouses here

Itasca Lofts

to be converted into housing. The plain red brick buildings to the north, which date to 1906, are also part of the complex and were originally known as the C and D warehouses.

35 Minnesota Opera Center (S. J. Cooke Co. warehouse) N L

620 First St. North

Frederick A. Clarke, 1892 / renovated, Phillips Klein Companies, 1990

Gaar Scott Historic Lofts (S. J. Cooke Co. warehouse) N L

614 First St. North

Frederick A. Clarke, 1892 / renovated, Paul Madson and Associates, 2001

These buildings offer two dramatic examples of historic preservation. The Gaar Scott Lofts—named after a farm implement manufacturer that once occupied the building—was for decades covered by a green metal screen. When the screen was finally removed, the effect was both startling and beautiful. The adjacent building that's now part of the Minnesota Opera Center suffered a fire that destroyed its interior, but architects were able to insert three floors of new space inside the shell while preserving the entire five-story facade.

Creamette Historic Lofts

36 River Station N L

First St. and Sixth Ave. North
(560 Second St. North)

J. Buxell Architecture, 1998–2002

One of the largest housing developments in Minneapolis history, consisting of 348 units in 12 buildings. Too bad, then, that it has so little architectural character. Instead, the buildings retreat behind timid brick shells, as though terrified of anything that smacks of modernity.

37 Creamette Historic Lofts (Champion Reaper Co. Warehouse) N L

428–32 First St. North

Long and Kees, 1897 / addition and renovation, Paul Madson and Associates, 1998

A fine Richardsonian Romanesque building. Dominating the composition is a magnificent sandstone arch, a staircase set within it, that makes for a most emphatic front

entrance. Originally an implement warehouse, the building was purchased in 1916 by what later became the Creamette Co., a pioneer in developing fast-cooking elbow macaroni (the secret lay in making the macaroni thinner and the hole in the middle larger). An addition was constructed in 1998 when the building was converted to housing.

38 Heritage Landing N L

415 First St. North

BKV Group, 2000 and later

With its neo-Victorian corner turret, mansard roof, brash colors, and general atmosphere of festive excess, this brazen confection—which includes a variety of housing units as well as retail space—is so close to pure pop architecture that you almost expect to see costumed Disney characters rappelling down the walls. Still, give this garish devil its due: at least it's got some life

Riverwalk Condominiums, 400 First St. North

and energy to it, which is more than can be said of the neutered brick boxes that too often pass for modern architecture elsewhere in the warehouse district.

39 Riverwalk Condominiums (Lindsay Brothers Building) N L

400 First St. North

Harry Jones, 1895, 1909 / renovated, Oertel Architects, 1987 / 2004

Riverwalk Condominiums (Chicago, St. Paul, Minneapolis and Omaha Railroad freight house) N L

50–56 Fourth Ave. North

1880–1928

The old Lindsay Brothers Building is another impressive design from Harry Jones, with especially fine brickwork along the cornice. Although it has Gothic-style windows, the building's overall design is reminiscent of H. H. Richardson's seminal Marshall Field Warehouse of 1887 in Chicago. It was constructed for Lindsay Brothers Co., a farm implement wholesaler. Converted to housing in 1987, the warehouse was renovated a second time in 2004 to create loft-style condominiums. A new building called **Lindsay Lofts** was constructed just to the north in 2001.

The Riverwalk complex also includes a brick freight house that was built for the Omaha Road. It's one of the largest railroad remnants in the warehouse district, where the Omaha and two other railways—the Northern Pacific and the Soo Line—once maintained tracks and large yards along First and Second Sts. North. These old rail corridors have now been almost completely filled in with new development.

40 Ribnick Furs (Berman Brothers) Building N L

224 First St. North

William D. Kimball, 1884 / addition, Jack Boarman, 1988

A delightful little building with oversized keystones that punctuate the second story like exclamation points.

41 Prisma International (Hennepin Hotel) N L

204 First St. North

1888

Chicago House N L

124 First St. North

Carl F. Struck, 1884

Foster House N L

100 First St. North

1882 / 1884 / 1886

A number of small hotels for workingmen were built along this part of First St. in the 1880s. These three charmers, all restored, are

Chicago House

Realty Co. Warehouse

recipient of two brilliant remodelings that came 90 years apart.
The first transformation was the
work of Cass Gilbert. Between

among the surviving examples.
The Chicago House is the most
elaborate of the trio, with banded
stonework and a typically busy
Victorian cornice.

42 Realty Co. Warehouse ! N L

106 First Ave. North (also 105
First St. North)

*Edward S. Stebbins, 1889 / re-
modeled, Cass Gilbert, 1902–6 /
remodeled, Paul Madson and
Associates, 1992*

One of the warehouse district's
outstanding buildings and the

1902 and 1906, Gilbert—then still
busy with his Minnesota State
Capitol—gave the warehouse a
Gothic makeover, unifying the
main facade with a series of
inset arches.

In 1992 Paul Madson and
Associates undertook an equally
superb intervention, converting
the cavernous warehouse, used
for cold storage for many years,
into a lively new space for Theatre
de la Jeune Lune. In July 2008,
after a 30-year-run, the theater
company disbanded, and at
last report the building was up
for sale.

3 The Central Riverfront

The Central Riverfront

For many decades, most of the central riverfront was the flour-dusted industrial heart of Minneapolis, a densely built environment of mills and factories powered by a subterranean maze of racing waterways. What made it all possible was St. Anthony Falls, where the Mississippi River in its natural state fell 75 feet through a mile-long tumult of cascades and rapids. The falls also happened to be in just the right place, poised between pineries to the north and prairies—ideal for growing grain—to the south and west. Although sawmilling initially flourished at the falls, flour millers soon became dominant as wheat poured in from farms along an ever expanding system of rail lines.

The first mills appeared along the western side of the falls in the 1820s, built by soldiers from Fort Snelling to grind flour and saw logs. But it wasn't until the 1850s, when the west bank opened to settlement and a power canal was excavated, that the flour milling industry began a period of astonishing growth. By the 1880s, 25 mills clustered along the west bank, forming one of the largest water-powered industrial complexes in human history. Railroad tracks threaded around and through the mills, some crossing the Mississippi on James J. Hill's Stone Arch Bridge, built in 1883. Meanwhile, subsidiary industries—including bag and barrel makers and manufacturers of milling machinery—sprang up nearby to feed the roaring colossus of flour.

The mills were of masonry construction, with heavy timber interior frames, and the largest of them, such as the Washburn A (1880, now Mill City Museum), could turn out over a million pounds of flour a day. Yet for all its might, the milling industry couldn't withstand the power of changing market forces that gradually ate away at Minneapolis's flour production in the early twentieth century. The west bank's first flour mill, the Cataract, closed in 1928, and more were shuttered in the 1930s when Buffalo, NY, became the nation's largest flour miller.

By the 1960s, when the last of the mills shut down, the falls area had become a landscape of loss and decay. But cities can be surprisingly resilient, and the seeds of an urban revolution were already in the air by 1971, when most of the old milling quarter was placed within the St. Anthony Falls Historic District. A wave of trendy redevelopment occurred in the 1980s, when several old mills—including the Standard (1879, now Whitney Landmark Residences) and the Crown Roller (1880, now offices)—were renovated with the aid of historic tax credits and large infusions of public money. The reopening of the Stone Arch Bridge in 1994 for pedestrian use was another milestone.

Around 2000 a second and much larger wave of development, fueled by a booming housing market, began to sweep through the district, utterly transforming it. Piece by piece, the old industrial order gave way to a new and decidedly upscale precinct of parks, museums, theaters, office buildings, restaurants, hotels, and apartments. The boom is over now, and in the chastening light of recession the riverfront has lost some of its luster, but there's no question that what happened here was a remarkable feat of urban revitalization.

The new and remodeled buildings that have now all but filled the district include the usual examples of tepid historicism, but some outstanding works of modern architecture can also be found here. Among the best are Meyer Scherer and Rockcastle's Mill City Museum (2003), carved from the burned-out hulk of the Washburn A Mill; the broodingly blue Guthrie Theater (2006), designed by the French architect Jean Nouvel; and Humboldt Lofts (1878), a mill converted to apartments in 2003 by Julie Snow Architects.

The Central Riverfront

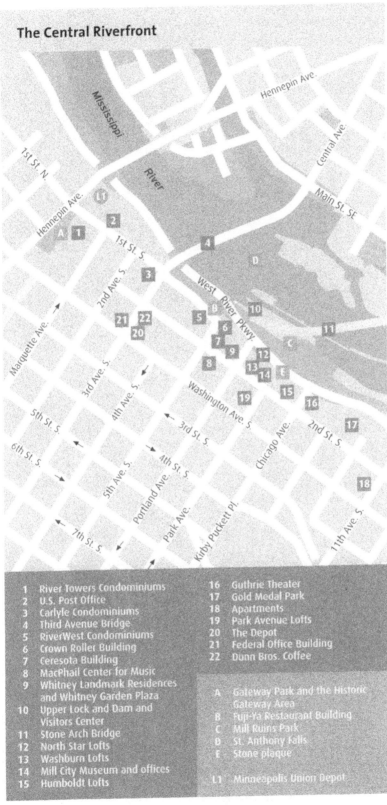

1   River Towers Condominiums
2   U.S. Post Office
3   Carlyle Condominiums
4   Third Avenue Bridge
5   RiverWest Condominiums
6   Crown Roller Building
7   Ceresota Building
8   MacPhail Center for Music
9   Whitney Landmark Residences
    and Whitney Garden Plaza
10 Upper Lock and Dam and
    Visitors Center
11 Stone Arch Bridge
12 North Star Lofts
13 Washburn Lofts
14 Mill City Museum and offices
15 Humboldt Lofts

16 Guthrie Theater
17 Gold Medal Park
18 Apartments
19 Park Avenue Lofts
20 The Depot
21 Federal Office Building
22 Dunn Bros. Coffee

A   Gateway Park and the Historic
    Gateway Area
B   Fuji-Ya Restaurant Building
C   Mill Ruins Park
D   St. Anthony Falls
E   Stone plaque

L1 Minneapolis Union Depot

POI A Gateway Park and the Historic Gateway Area N L

South and east of First St. and Hennepin Ave.

Minneapolis Park Board, 1963

Today's Gateway Park, a bland plaza from the 1960s, is nothing like the first park built here in 1915. That park, which occupied a triangle between Hennepin and Nicollet Aves., was known for its pavilion, a classical structure with curving, colonnaded wings.

The park and pavilion were fruits of the so-called City Beautiful movement of the early 1900s. The idea was to create monumental streets, buildings, and parks that would express the grandeur of American civilization while clearing away Victorian-era detritus. It was, in other words, a high-minded species of urban renewal. In fact, two blocks of old buildings, among them the first **Minneapolis City Hall** (1873), were demolished for the original Gateway Park.

But the park failed to transform the larger Gateway area, which by the 1950s had become the city's undisputed skid row, home to a floating population of impoverished men served by bars, liquor stores, flophouses, and second-hand shops. The pavilion came down in 1953, while the park itself was rebuilt after urban renewal had cleared away much of the historic Gateway. About 180 buildings, most from the nineteenth century, were razed for the Gateway urban renewal project and replaced by modern structures or parking lots. Today, about the only reminder of the historic park is the **George Washington Memorial Flagstaff.** Now located near First and Hennepin, it features an elaborate base designed by Daniel Chester French and was installed in the old park in 1917.

1 River Towers Condominiums N L

15–19 First St. South

John Pruyn, 1964 / renovated, Close Associates, 2004

A dull apartment tower of the kind thought to be the height of fashion in the 1960s.

2 U.S. Post Office N L

100 First St. South

Magney and Tusler (Leon Arnal), 1934 / addition and remodeling, HGA, 1991

A very good art deco building in a bad place, cutting off access to the riverfront for three blocks along First St. In the 1930s, however, the building's location made perfect sense, providing direct access to the rail lines that then

U.S. Post Office

Third Avenue Bridge

delivered much of the nation's mail. As built, the post office was fronted along First by Pioneer Square Park. The park was lost to urban renewal in the 1960s, and an apartment building now occupies its site, obscuring distant views of the post office's monumental facade.

The post office, designed by the same architects responsible for the Foshay Tower, displays an art deco–classical blend characteristic of the 1930s. Sheathed in Mankato-Kasota stone, the building stages a long, rhythmic march down First, the broad piers and inset windows of its lower three floors producing the effect of a classic colonnade. The stepped-back fourth story and blocky corner entrances, however, are art deco hallmarks. Inside, there's a block-long, virtually pristine art deco lobby outfitted with marble walls and much brasswork. The brass light fixture that runs the length of the lobby is said to be the longest in the country.

LOST 1 *Before the post office was constructed, much of its site was occupied by the* **Minneapolis Union Depot,** *which opened in 1885. The depot stood until 1914, when the much larger* **Great Northern Depot** *(also gone) was built just across Hennepin.*

3 Carlyle Condominiums N L

100 Third Ave. South

Humphreys and Partners Architects (Dallas), 2007

At 39 stories, this is the tallest residential tower in Minneapolis. The style appears to mix faux classicism with hints of art deco.

4 Third Avenue Bridge N L

Across Mississippi River

Concrete Steel Engineering Co. (New York), Frederick Cappelen, and Kristoffer Oustad, 1914–18 / renovated, Loren Pierce and Conrad Wurm (engineers), 1980

Spanning St. Anthony Falls, this bridge's graceful double curve stems from a happy convergence of form and function. The curve was dictated by the need to place four river piers just so in order to avoid holes in the limestone ledge at the falls. Renovated in 1980, the bridge is the oldest of five concrete-arch spans that cross the Mississippi between St. Anthony Falls and the Ford Dam.

5 RiverWest Condominiums N L

401 First St. South

KKE Architects, 1989 / renovated, 2004

A long, 18-story-high wall between downtown and the river and a depressing example of how not to build housing at water's edge.

Carlyle Condominiums

POI B Fuji-Ya Restaurant Building N L

420 First St. South

Shinichi Okada and Newton Griffith, 1968

This small building, constructed atop mill ruins, was among the first attempts to bring new life to the downtown riverfront. The restaurant, owned by Reiko Weston, was forced to close after the Minneapolis Park Board acquired much of the site by eminent domain in 1987.

Crown Roller Building

6 Crown Roller Building (Crown Roller Mill) N L

105 Fifth Ave. South

W. F. Gunn (engineer), 1880 / addition (boiler house), 1908 / renovated, Architectural Alliance, 1986

With its mansard roof, this may be the handsomest of the old mill buildings around the falls, although much of what you see today is a reconstruction. Operating until the early 1950s, it was one of the last mills to close on the west bank. A fire in 1983 destroyed the interior and roof of the vacant structure, and for a time it looked as though it would be torn down. Preservationists convinced the city to save what remained, however, and in 1986 the old mill—with a new interior and new roof—reopened as an office building.

7 Ceresota Building (Northwestern Consolidated Elevator A) N L

155 Fifth Ave. South

G. T. Honstain (engineer), 1908 / renovated, Ellerbe Becket, 1988

An old brick grain elevator converted into offices arranged around a new atrium. The large Ceresota sign—identifying a former owner of the elevator—was preserved as part of the renovation.

8 MacPhail Center for Music

501 Second St. South

James Dayton Design, 2008

A spiffy new $25 million home for the MacPhail Center for Music, which was founded as a violin school in 1907 and now offers a wide variety of education and performance programs. The building is organized into two sections. A cube faced in Cor-Ten steel holds down the corner and includes classrooms as well as a 225-seat concert hall. Wrapped around the cube is an angular six-story office and studio wing sheathed in over 7,000 zinc panels. A glassy lobby joins the two parts. Overall, it's a crisp design—nothing especially fancy, but

MacPhail Center for Music

more interesting than most of the new architecture along the riverfront. The building's overall form and its use of metal surfaces show the influence of California architect Frank Gehry's work (visible just downriver at the Weisman Art Museum on the University of Minnesota campus). This connection is no accident: architect James Dayton worked in Gehry's office for five years.

Whitney Landmark Residences

9 Whitney Landmark Residences (Standard Mill) and Whitney Garden Plaza N L

150 Portland Ave.

W. D. Gray, 1879 / renovated, Miller, Hanson, Westerbeck and Bell, 1988 / renovated, Tanek Architects, 2006

Built by Dorilus Morrison, Minneapolis's first mayor, this brick mill was one of the last to come equipped with millstones as well as rollers to grind flour. It closed in the 1940s. The long-vacant mill was converted into a luxury hotel in the 1980s, which is also when the adjoining plaza and its giant chessboard were completed. In 2006 the building was renovated a second time, into condominiums.

10 Upper Lock and Dam and Visitors Center N L

1 Portland Ave.

U.S. Army Corps of Engineers, 1963

Although the suspicion persists that the Upper Lock and Dam project was federal pork at its most succulent, it did produce this solid piece of 1960s industrial architecture. The lookout area atop the visitor center offers a fine view of the falls as well as information about its history.

POI C Mill Ruins Park ! N L

First St. South and Portland Ave.

URS Corp., 2001 and later

This park is a three-dimensional map of a lost world, offering a cutaway view of the complex engineering that underlay the west side milling district. The ruins—a maze of building foundations, walls, tunnels, and pits—were uncovered in 2001 after being hidden for years beneath fill excavated during construction of the St. Anthony Falls Lock and Dam in the 1960s.

The key to the milling district was a canal built in 1857 and later enlarged twice. Fourteen feet deep, the canal (long since filled in) extended 900 feet beneath First St. Taking in water at a gatehouse above the falls, the canal ran to the eastern end of the Washburn milling complex. The canal itself was excavated from limestone, but beneath it ran a deep layer of sandstone ideal for

Mill Ruins Park

Central Riverfront

tunneling. As a result, tailrace tunnels leading back to the Mississippi could be dug beneath the power canal, allowing mills to operate on both sides. At most other water power sites, such as those in New England, mills could be built only on a canal's river side.

By the 1860s, mills lined the canal, gulping water to power turbines lodged at the bottom of wheel pits. Dropping by as much as 40 feet, the water created such force that a single turbine could drive all of a mill's machinery. After serving its purpose, the water was sent back to the river via tailrace tunnels and a main tailrace channel that is now the park's centerpiece.

The park includes ruins of several mills, among them the Minneapolis Mill (built in 1865), the Pillsbury B Mill (1866), the Excelsior Mill (1870), and the Northwestern Mill (1879). Most of these mills were demolished in the early 1930s, though the Excelsior survived until 1961.

POI D St. Anthony Falls

includes **Falls of St. Anthony (Upper) Dam**, *Charles H. Bigelow (engineer), 1858 / many later modifications and improvements*

Although no match for Niagara, St. Anthony Falls in its natural state—set amid rolling prairies and patches of woodland—must have been one of the great spectacles of the continent. Today, after nearly two centuries of industrial use, almost every natural feature of the falls has been

obliterated or altered. Before dams, tunnels, channels, canals, spillways, walls, and other structures harnessed the power of the falls, the Mississippi poured over a 16-foot-high limestone ledge, then roared through a series of rapids into the only gorge on its 2,500-mile-long course. Because the river level has been raised by dams below the falls, the rapids are no longer visible. The last major construction project at the falls occurred in the 1960s, when the U.S. Army Corps of Engineers built the Upper Lock and Dam. This allowed barges and other river traffic to navigate past the falls—long a dream of Minneapolis boosters.

11 Stone Arch Bridge ! N ﹏ ⅃

Across Mississippi River below St. Anthony Falls

Charles C. Smith (engineer), 1883 / two spans replaced, U.S. Army Corps of Engineers, 1963 / renovated, Minnesota Department of Transportation and A. J. Lichtenstein and Associates (New York), 1994

The most poetic of all Twin Cities bridges and a spectacular feat of Victorian engineering. Sweeping across the river at a diagonal and then curving to follow the western shore, the 2,100-foot-long structure is the Mississippi's only stone arch bridge. It's also the second-oldest railroad bridge (next to the 1874 Eads Bridge in St. Louis) on the river. Since reopening as a pedestrian bridge in 1994, it's become a sturdy

St. Anthony Falls

Stone Arch Bridge, 1942

symbol of the reinvigorated milling district.

The bridge, designated a National Engineering Landmark in 2000, was built by James J. Hill, who called it "the hardest thing I ever had to do in my life." He needed the bridge to bring his St. Paul, Minneapolis and Manitoba Railroad (predecessor of the Great Northern) into downtown Minneapolis. Scoffers called the project "Jim Hill's folly," pointing to the difficulty of constructing a bridge of any kind—let alone a curving stone bridge with 23 arches—across the treacherous waters below St. Anthony Falls. Despite its difficult site, Hill's "folly" was finished in less than two years, consuming 100,000 tons of stone, including limestone quarried on site. Over 300 men a day toiled on the project (for an average daily wage of $1.25), and the work was often dangerous, especially in the winter months. A least three men died during construction.

When the bridge opened in November 1883, even the skeptics had to admit it was a work of rare magnificence. The bridge, with some modifications—including the replacement of two arches with a steel truss in the 1960s to provide clearance for the new lock at St. Anthony Falls—carried Great Northern trains across the river until 1978. In 1992 the State of Minnesota acquired the bridge and over the next two years renovated it for use as a pedestrian span.

Today, a walk across the bridge, which received dramatic new lighting in 2005, is one of the great experiences of the city, offering an unmatched vista of St. Anthony Falls and the milling district as well as the tactile pleasure of feeling beneath your feet a structure truly built for the ages.

12 North Star Lofts (North Star Woolen Mill) N *L*

117 Portland Ave.

1864 / addition, ca. 1885–90 / addition, Pike and Cook, 1922 / old portion rebuilt, C. F. Haglin and Sons, 1925 / renovated, Paul Madson and Associates, 1999 / addition (Stone Arch Lofts), Paul Madson Associates with LHB Architects, 2001

Although it was almost entirely rebuilt in 1925, portions of this building date back to the North Star Mill's founding in 1864. At least two other textile mills were established at St. Anthony Falls in the 1860s, but the North Star was the only one left by 1885. The mill specialized in wool blankets and for many years supplied them to the Pullman Co. for use in its railway cars.

The rebuilding and enlargement of the old section in 1925 was unusual in that it was done from the top down. The project began with construction of a new floor above the existing roof. Machinery was then moved up from the floor below, after which that floor was rebuilt. This process continued down to the ground floor, allowing the factory to operate during the entire period of reconstruction. Closed in the late 1940s, the mill was later used as a warehouse. The conversion to condominiums was skillfully accomplished in 1999. A new section to the rear of the building, known as the Stone Arch Lofts, was added in 2001.

13 Washburn Lofts (Washburn Utility Building) N L

700 Second St. South

Hewitt and Brown, 1914 / renovated, Paul Madson and Associates and LHB Architects, 2001 / Art: terra-cotta figures (atop Second St. side of building), John Karl Daniels, 1914

Now apartments, this industrial building originally included shops and offices serving the A mill complex. The terra-cotta figures high on the Second St. facade show milling techniques through the ages. The figures on the left and right depict men grinding grain by hand, while the larger central figure tends to a mechanized roller of the kind used in modern mills.

Washburn A Mill Complex
! N ⋆ L

Second St. South between Park and Chicago Aves.

various architects and engineers, 1880–1928

This is hallowed industrial ground and one of the most significant historic sites in the Twin Cities. It includes portions of what was, when built, the largest flour mill in the world. Using novel techniques to grind high-grade flour from hard spring wheat, the A mill helped put Minneapolis on the world map. At least nine structures once comprised the complex, which included elevators, engine houses, a wheelhouse, a wheat house, and a small office building.

The mill's concrete grain elevators, built between 1906 and 1928, were especially fascinating to European *avant garde* architects like Le Corbusier, who viewed them as pure examples of modern functionalist design. Architectural historian Reyner Banham, in his 1986 book *A Concrete Atlantis*, wrote that "it could be argued, and with very little exaggeration, that Elevators A, B, and C of the Washburn-Crosby complex constitute the most internationally influential structures ever put up in North America."

The man behind the mill was Cadwallader Washburn, a Maine-born entrepreneur who with his brother William got in on the ground floor of the flour milling business around St. Anthony Falls. He built his first mill here in the 1860s. In 1874, fresh from a stint as governor of Wisconsin, Washburn constructed a second and larger mill, known as the A (his earlier mill next door was renamed the B). Despite its massive stone walls, the first A mill had a short life. On May 2, 1878, the structure was literally blown to pieces in an explosion that claimed the lives of 18 workers and damaged or destroyed five adjoining mills.

Washburn and his partner, John Crosby, made immediate plans to rebuild but first had to fight a court battle with their insurance company, which claimed that the mill was covered against fire but not explosion. Washburn's lawyers were able to prove that a fire caused the explosion and not the other way around, and the insurance company paid up.

The new A mill, completed in 1880, was also built of stone, but it incorporated many advances in milling technology that made it far superior to its doomed predecessor. Rollers were used instead of stones to grind the flour, and the mill also came equipped with middlings purifiers, devices that removed all traces of bran from hard spring wheat, thereby producing a perfectly white, if notably fiber deficient, flour. Powered by twin turbines, the mill could turn out over a million pounds of flour a day. The A mill complex ground flour until 1965, when it was shut down by General Mills, the successor firm of the Washburn Crosby Co. A sign advertising the firm's "gold medal" flour still stands atop a grain elevator that forms part of the complex.

The mill, with much of its historic machinery intact, stood vacant for the next quarter century. Then, in 1991, a fire—probably set by homeless people—all but destroyed the structure.

Mill City Museum

Fortunately, portions of the walls survived, and they were eventually stabilized as part of a plan to create a museum in what remained of the mill. Today, Washburn's mill and its auxiliary buildings serve new purposes but remain a centerpiece of the milling district.

14 Mill City Museum and offices (Washburn A Mill and Wheat House) !

A Mill, 704 Second St. South

Adolph Fischer and William de la Barre (engineers), 1880 / rebuilt after fire, 1928 / interior destroyed by fire, 1991

Wheat House, 710 Second St. South

Adolph Fischer and William de la Barre (engineers), 1881 / rebuilt after fire, 1928 / interior destroyed by fire, 1991

Mill City Museum

renovation and new construction, MS&R Architects, 2003

This dazzling example of historic renovation refutes the misguided notion that the best way to honor the past is to imitate it. Instead, modern and historic architecture are intertwined here in a way that honors both. At the heart of the project is the Mill City Museum, operated by the Minnesota Historical Society and devoted to telling the story of the flour industry.

In designing the museum to fit within the derelict and fire-devastated A mill complex, architect Thomas Meyer of Meyer Scherer and Rockcastle in Minneapolis wisely avoided trying to create any kind of nostalgic pastiche. He left the exteriors of the old mill and wheat house largely intact while creating new spaces within, including the museum and four floors of office space above. But Meyer and his team also made a bold modern statement, inserting a glass-walled structure into the oldest and most heavily damaged portion of the mill. The remainder of the ruins was then left open to form a walled courtyard.

The design works brilliantly, glass playing off against stone something in the manner of I. M. Pei's celebrated pyramid at the Louvre in Paris, so that the museum manages to be at once rigorously modern and highly romantic—a rare combination. Inside, the museum features a spacious lobby with an intriguing wooden ceiling scrim, a variety of exhibit spaces, and a ride known as the "flour tower" that provides an interpretive history of the milling industry. Meyer's design also ensures that museumgoers have an excellent view of the biggest exhibit of all—the old mill itself.

POI E Stone plaque

Above the entrance to the Mill City Museum's plaza, First St. South

This plaque, dating to 1880, commemorates the 14 "faithful and well tried employees" killed in the May 2, 1878, explosion of the first A mill. Four men working in neighboring mills also died in the blast, which was so powerful that it lifted the mill's roof by 200 feet and hurled chunks of stone up to eight blocks away. It remains the worst industrial accident in the city's history.

15 Humboldt Lofts (Humboldt Mill)

750 Second St. South

J. T. Noyes and Sons, 1878 / addition, 1913 / renovated and enlarged, Julie Snow Architects, 2003

The historic portion of these apartments was built in 1878 as the Humboldt Mill, which later became the Washburn E Mill. Architect Julie Snow designed a crisp addition to the long-vacant mill as part of its conversion to 36 loft-style condominiums. The two-level units are interlocked, an ingenious trick first used by the architect Le Corbusier in the 1940s for an apartment block in France.

16 Guthrie Theater ! N L

818 Second St. South

Jean Nouvel (Paris) with Architectural Alliance, 2006

Large, dark, and rather mysterious, this new riverfront landmark is like a play full of wonderful moments that doesn't quite achieve its full dramatic potential. It's drawn plenty of comparisons to Ralph Rapson's groundbreaking 1963 theater for the Guthrie. That theater was small, funky, and rather cheaply built— not quite a flower child, perhaps, but possessing some of that old hippie spirit. The new Guthrie, by contrast, conveys a sense of mass and power, so much so that you could image real electricity, as opposed to the theatrical kind, being generated here.

The Guthrie is French architect Jean Nouvel's first completed work in the United States, and what may be most impressive about it is how well he and his team (including the Architectural Alliance of Minneapolis)

Guthrie Theater, Second St. South entrance

Guthrie Theater, West River Parkway entrance

responded to the site. The theater's proximity to the Washburn A Mill was not lost on Nouvel, and it explains the Guthrie's robustly industrial look. A gentle, delicate building simply would not have worked on this site.

The building's midnight blue skin, which displays screen-printed images from old Guthrie plays, has provoked much discussion. It is indeed a startling color choice. But if you keep in mind that the Guthrie is in many ways a building designed to celebrate the night, a sort of architectural nocturne, then the color makes sense.

Inside, Nouvel's design is less compelling. To be sure, the three performance spaces—a thrust-stage theater virtually identical to Rapson's original, a proscenium theater, and a small "studio" for experimental works—are well done. The studio also has the building's coolest space: an "amber box" lobby that provides stunning views of the riverfront. On the other hand, what passes for the Guthrie's main entrance lobby is a hallwaylike room of no architectural distinction. To reach the theaters, you have to ride long, walled-in escalators that are as likely to induce claustrophobia as anticipation. On the second floor you'll discover more wide hallways doing double duty as lobbies. The overall tone of these quasi lobbies is so noirish that in places you'll almost feel as though you've wandered into some wise guys' hangout in New Jersey.

The building's peculiar circulation patterns were dictated in part by its most dramatic feature—a long cantilevered walkway (called the "endless bridge,") that projects out toward the river in a way that necessitates a central crossroads on the second floor. During intermissions, this congested crossing becomes a kind of forced mixer, which is apparently what Nouvel had in mind. If the bridge delivered some fabulous benefit, it might have been worth all the trouble, but in truth the view from its small open-air balcony isn't significantly better than if Nouvel had simply created a large window on the river side of the theater.

All that said, the Guthrie is a strong design that never fails to be interesting, even when it's most irritating. It's the kind of building that inspires curiosity: if you walk by, you'll want to step inside to see what all the fuss is about. That's not a bad thing. The Guthrie's directors wanted a new building that would provide the theater with an unmistakable architectural identity, and Nouvel's design—whether you like it or not—does just that.

17 Gold Medal Park N L

Second St. and 11th Ave. South

Oslund and Associates, 2007

A small park that features a 32-foot-high mound built up from contaminated soil on the site and capped with four feet of clean fill. Inspired by Indian burial sites along the Mississippi, the mound has a mysterious presence, and the park is one of the most evocative public spaces along the downtown riverfront.

Apartments, 212 11th Ave. South

18 Apartments (Ida Dorsey Brothel)

212 11th Ave. South

1891

Minneapolis once had a flourishing red light district along the downtown riverfront. Most of the old houses of ill repute are long gone, but this Romanesque Revival building—once the city's most elegant temple of passion—has somehow survived urban renewal.

19 Park Avenue Lofts

200 Park Ave.

Julie Snow Architects, 2005

Milwaukee Road tracks once ran here between Second St. and Washington Ave., but new construction has filled in much of the old rail corridor. These well-designed, two-story apartments are among the latest additions to the area.

20 The Depot ! N i

225 Third Ave. South

Milwaukee Road Depot, Charles S. Frost (Chicago), 1899 / renovated, ESG Architects and Shea Architects, 2001

Courtyard by Marriott and Residence Inn, ESG Architects, 2001

Once the Milwaukee Road Depot, this stately old brick and granite building has found new life as a hotel and event center, while its historically significant iron train shed now shelters an ice skating rink. Redevelopment did not come easily. After the depot closed in 1971, reuse schemes came and went in a cloud of bankruptcies and foreclosures, and it wasn't until 2001 that the old depot—joined by a pair of modestly designed hotels—finally reopened in its new guise.

The Milwaukee Road built its first depot here (where the train shed now stands) in 1876. By the mid-1890s the railroad hired Chicago architect Charles Frost to design a new depot. Frost, who would later go on to design St. Paul's Union Depot (1923) and the Great Northern Station (1914, gone) in Minneapolis, produced a Renaissance Revival–style building with a pinnacled clock tower modeled on that of the Giralda in Seville, Spain. Unfortunately, high winds ruined the ornate pinnacle in 1941, leaving the tower with the

The Depot

unsatisfactory flat top it retains to this day.

Within, the waiting room—now known as the Great Hall—included marble floors, arched doorways, and a decorative plaster ceiling. The depot's real glory, however, was its 625-foot-long iron train shed. Up to 29 trains a day once idled beneath the shed, which had four openings in the roof to vent locomotive smoke. Now used for parking as well as skating (behind a new glass curtain wall), the iron shed is one of only about a dozen such structures believed to remain in the United States.

21 Federal Office Building (U.S. Post Office)

220 Washington Ave. South (212 Third Ave. South)

Supervising Architect of the U.S. Treasury (James Knox Taylor), 1915 / renovated, 1927

A solid specimen of Beaux-Arts classicism, with an impressive two-story-high colonnade done in the rather exotic Roman composite order. Designed as a U.S. post office, the building never worked especially well for that purpose. It was converted to a federal office building in 1937, not long after a new main post office opened two blocks away. The Selective Service System had its offices here, and the building was the scene of protests during the Vietnam War era as well as a 1970 bombing that caused extensive damage near the Second St. entrance.

22 Dunn Bros. Coffee (Milwaukee Road Freight House) N L

201 Third Ave. South

Charles Haglin, 1879 / rear portion demolished, 1989 / front portion renovated, Design Partnership, 1998

This two-story brick building was originally the front of a freight house serving the Milwaukee Road Depot. The rear was demolished in 1989, and two modern hotels now occupy the site.

Federal Office Building

4 Downtown East and Elliot Park

Downtown East and Elliot Park

These adjoining neighborhoods have quite different architectural characters. Downtown East, perhaps best known today as home to the Hubert H. Humphrey Metrodome (1982), developed largely as an industrial and warehousing district, especially along Washington Avenue and Third Street South. Many of Downtown East's old buildings, including the superb Thresher Square (1900, 1904) and the equally fine American Trio Lofts (1911) have been renovated for housing or offices. The opening of the Hiawatha Light Rail Line will likely spur even more development here in years to come.

By contrast, Elliot Park is a classic mixed-use neighborhood, occupying an intermediate zone between downtown and residential districts to the south. It has a diverse array of buildings, from residential and medical high-rises to walk-up apartments to a scattering of single-family homes. Situated at a point where the city's downtown and main north-south grids collide, Elliot Park also offers a pleasing jumble of streets. Skewed intersections and oddly shaped building lots abound here, and it's one of the few places in the city where you can easily lose your sense of direction.

Elliot Park derives its name from a small, irregularly shaped park on a site donated to the city in 1883 by Dr. Jacob Elliot, a local physician. Like other neighborhoods around the edges of downtown, Elliot Park—which began to be settled in the 1850s—was at first largely residential, with Swedish immigrants predominating. By the 1870s, however, commercial and institutional uses began to change the neighborhood's character. St. Barnabas Hospital opened on Seventh Street South in 1871. Later, Asbury, Abbott, and Swedish hospitals located nearby. These early hospitals either are gone or have relocated, but the Hennepin County Medical Center—an outgrowth of the old General Hospital, founded in 1887—remains an important institutional presence in Elliot Park. So, too, does North Central University, which occupies the former site of Asbury Hospital.

As commercial and institutional uses pushed farther south into the neighborhood in the 1880s and 1890s, apartment buildings and row houses began to replace much of the original housing stock. A surprising number of Elliot Park's Victorian-era apartment structures have survived, and many are now preserved within the city-designated South Ninth Street Historic District. Today, apartments still dominate the neighborhood, although a few single-family homes can still be found south of 14th Street.

The construction of Interstates 94 and 35W in the 1960s swept away the southern fringes of Elliot Park, destroying many homes and apartments, and the neighborhood lost over half its population from 1950 to 1970. Residents who remained were mostly very poor and lived in crowded apartment buildings. One old row house, for example, had 53 apartments carved out of only seven original units.

Elliot Park began to rebound in the 1970s, fueled by community groups that renovated old housing and built new homes as well. The population decline was stemmed, and the neighborhood is now growing again, in part because of an infusion of Somali immigrants. Recent housing projects—such as the East Village (2001) and Grant Park Condominiums and City Homes (2004)—have further revitalized the neighborhood.

In addition to the South Ninth Street Historic District, Elliot Park's architectural highlights include the Hinkle-Murphy House (1887), the First Church of Christ Scientist (1897), the art deco–style Minneapolis Armory (1936), and the delightful Band Box Diner, a neighborhood institution since 1939.

POI A Elliot Park

1000 14th St. East

*ca. 1880s and later / **recreation center**, 1960s / remodeled and enlarged, Bentz/Thompson/ Rietow Architects, 1982*

An oasis set amid institutional and residential buildings. The recreation center, which sports a conical roof, is a strong postmodern design from a firm—Bentz/ Thompson/Rietow—that does this sort of thing better than anyone else in the Twin Cities.

1 North Central University

910 Elliot Ave. South

Originally the North Central Bible Institute, this university was founded in 1930 and relocated here six years later, moving into what had been Asbury Hospital's main building. The university has since spread into a dozen or so other buildings, old and new, clustered around Elliot Park.

2 I. O. Miller Hall (Asbury Hospital)

910 Elliot Ave. South

Edwin P. Overmire, 1906 / 1916

A stately brick institutional building that extends for a full block

along the west side of Elliot Park. As designed, it included a dome above its central pavilion, which now terminates abruptly in a flat roof. Although it's modestly detailed, the building, with its symmetrical wings and arched entry, conveys a sense of quiet dignity.

The building opened in 1906 as the new home of Asbury Hospital but wasn't completed for another ten years due to financial problems. The hospital had been founded in 1892 by Sarah Harrison Knight, who named it after her father, Minneapolis businessman Thomas Asbury Harrison. Intended to serve indigent patients, the hospital was largely staffed by deaconesses from local Methodist churches. Asbury (now known as Methodist Hospital) later relocated to the suburbs.

3 T. J. Jones Information Resource Center (Tourtellotte Memorial Deaconess Home)

915 14th St. East

1915

Dr. Joseph Tourtellotte donated $125,000 to Asbury Hospital for the construction of this Georgian Revival–style building. At one

I. O. Miller Hall

Downtown East and Elliot Park

A   Elliot Park
B   Franklin Steele Square
C   South Ninth Street Historic District

L1   William and Mary Judd House

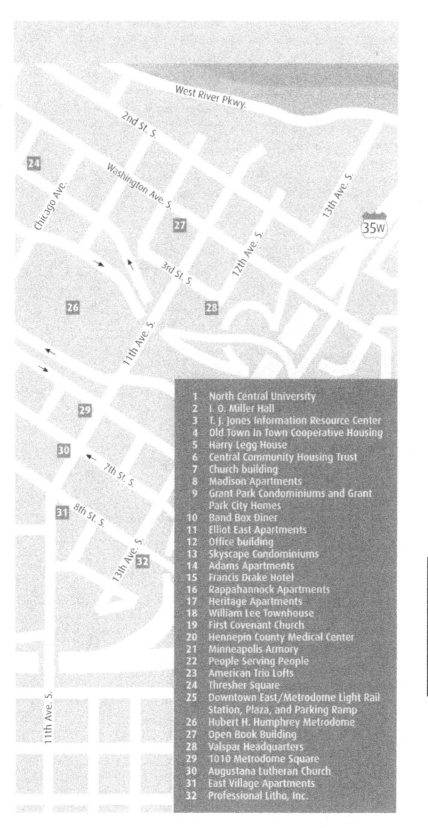

1   North Central University
2   I. O. Miller Hall
3   T. J. Jones Information Resource Center
4   Old Town In Town Cooperative Housing
5   Harry Legg House
6   Central Community Housing Trust
7   Church building
8   Madison Apartments
9   Grant Park Condominiums and Grant
    Park City Homes
10 Band Box Diner
11 Elliot East Apartments
12 Office building
13 Skyscape Condominiums
14 Adams Apartments
15 Francis Drake Hotel
16 Rappahannock Apartments
17 Heritage Apartments
18 William Lee Townhouse
19 First Covenant Church
20 Hennepin County Medical Center
21 Minneapolis Armory
22 People Serving People
23 American Trio Lofts
24 Thresher Square
25 Downtown East/Metrodome Light Rail
    Station, Plaza, and Parking Ramp
26 Hubert H. Humphrey Metrodome
27 Open Book Building
28 Valspar Headquarters
29 1010 Metrodome Square
30 Augustana Lutheran Church
31 East Village Apartments
32 Professional Litho, Inc.

Downtown East

time as many as 60 deaconesses lived here. It now serves as North Central's library.

4 Old Town In Town Cooperative Housing (Linne Flats) *L*

728, 732, 735, 736, 740 16th St. East

Frederick A. Clarke, 1892 / renovated

Five red brick apartment buildings converted into cooperative housing. Today they're part of the South Ninth Street Historic District.

Harry Legg House

5 Harry Legg House N *L*

1601 Park Ave. South

George H. Hoit and Co. (builder), 1887

Although Harry Legg is a name rich in comic possibilities, the first owner of this dandy Queen Anne house obviously didn't let it slow him down on the road to success: he later built a larger home on Lake of the Isles. This house is one of only a few Victorian-era single-family homes that survive in Elliot Park.

6 Central Community Housing Trust

1625 Park Ave. South

1962

The 1960s abounded in small buildings with big ideas. This is one of them. The roof flutters like a butterfly, the brick walls seem to fly out from the foundation, and the windows come in just about every size and shape except regular.

7 Church building (First Church of Christ Scientist) N *L*

614–20 15th St. East

Septimus J. Bowler, 1897 / addition, Septimus J. Bowler, 1899

Now in a state of ivied decrepitude, this brick church was the first Christian Science church building in the Upper Midwest. Founded by Mary Baker Eddy of Boston in 1879, the Christian Science movement spread quickly. By 1910 there were already seven Christian Science churches in Minneapolis.

London-born architect Septimus J. Bowler freely adapted forms from Roman and Renaissance models in designing the church, which has a Doric portico, brickwork coursed to imitate the rusticated look of stone, and terra-cotta trim. Within, the church featured an octagonal auditorium lit by large stained-glass windows, corner galleries, and a central plaster dome.

The Christian Scientists moved into a new, larger church at 24th St. and Nicollet Ave. in 1914. This building has been vacant since the 1980s, and its future is uncertain.

8 Madison Apartments (Madison School) *L*

501 15th St. East

Walter S. Pardee, 1887 / 1889 / renovated, 1980s

One of the city's oldest public school buildings, converted to apartments in the 1980s. Built of local brick, the building mixes Romanesque-style arched entries with Queen Anne detailing.

POI B Franklin Steele Square

Near 15th St. East and Portland Ave.

ca. 1882

Land for this small park was donated to the city in 1882 by the daughters of Minneapolis pioneer Franklin Steele.

Grant Park Condominiums

9 Grant Park Condominiums and Grant Park City Homes

500 Grant St. East

Humphreys and Partners Architects (Dallas) and Opus Architects and Engineers, 2004

A 27-story condominium tower with 39 townhomes spread around it in accord with the "new urbanist" bible. The townhomes strive to imitate the Romanesque Revival architecture of the nearby South Ninth Street Historic District but come across as a cartoon version of the real thing.

10 Band Box Diner *L*

729 Tenth St. South

Bert Wyman (Butler Manufacturing Co., builder), 1939 / renovated and enlarged, Robert Roscoe (Design for Preservation) and Karen Gjerstad, 2003

The oldest operating diner in Minneapolis and a beloved neighborhood landmark. Although modeled on the White Castle chain

of burger joints, the Band Box is a homegrown product. Harry Wyman and his wife, Bert, opened the diner—their first—in 1939. By 1950 they'd created a hamburger mini-empire of 15 Band Boxes, including four others in the downtown area. The diners, among the first in the city to be open 24 hours a day, featured a signature special—three hamburgers for a dime.

Bert Wyman is credited with designing the vaguely Modernestyle diner, which is built out of steel panels, allowing it to be easily disassembled and moved if need be. The Wymans sold the Band Box chain in 1953 at the height of its success. In the 1960s, competition from fast-food chains along with a population shift to the suburbs doomed many oldtime eateries. By 1972 all the Band Boxes were gone except for this one. New owners bought the diner in 1998 and later renovated and expanded it.

POI C South Ninth Street Historic District *L*

Ninth and Tenth Sts. South between Fifth Ave. South and Chicago Ave.

1989

This district, which is focused along Ninth St. but includes individual buildings as far south as 16th St., showcases some of the oldest row houses and apartments in Minneapolis. Built in response to the city's phenomenal growth in the 1880s and

Band Box Diner

1890s, the apartments here initially served a fairly wealthy clientele. Later, however, most were subdivided to accommodate a poorer class of tenants. In the 1980s, gentrification produced yet another change in the neighborhood's social dynamics: today, many of the apartments are upscale condominiums.

11 Elliot East Apartments (Potter Thompson Row Houses) *L*

812–26 Tenth St. South

Frederick A. Clarke, 1888

Now used as student housing by North Central University, this row house occupies a distinctive trapezoidal lot. Everything about the building, from its lot to the way its windows are arranged, is a bit odd.

12 Office building (Hinkle-Murphy House) N *L*

619 Tenth St. South

William Channing Whitney, 1887 / renovated, HKA Architects and Design for Preservation, 1997

One of downtown's last surviving mansions, and the first example of the Georgian Revival style (a variation of Colonial Revival) in Minneapolis. Built of structural tile and brick with stone trim, the Hinkle-Murphy House features a double-bowed front of the kind architect William Channing Whitney would have seen in Boston, where he trained before arriving in Minneapolis in the 1870s. Compared to the rambunctious Queen Anne houses still popular in the 1880s, this house must have seemed very quiet.

The mansion was built for businessman William Hinkle, whose interests included the Humboldt Flour Mill at St. Anthony Falls. It was purchased in 1901 by William Murphy, publisher of the Minneapolis *Tribune*. He lived in it until his death in 1918. The house is now used for offices.

13 Skyscape Condominiums

929 Portland Ave.

Built Form Architects (Chicago) and Cuningham Group, 2007

A 27-story condominium tower with 252 units and retail space on the ground floor. The building's name is more imaginative than its architecture.

14 Adams (Williston) Apartments *L*

500 Tenth St. South

Frederick A. Clarke, 1888

The first apartment building (as opposed to row house) in the district, built of red brick with sandstone trim. The arched entries are Renaissance Revival in character, but the turrets and arched windows above suggest the Romanesque.

15 Francis Drake Hotel

416 Tenth St. South

1926

Hotels with names familiar to older Minneapolitans—the Leamington, the Curtis, the Sheridan—once clustered along and near Tenth St. just to the west of here. The Drake, a center court design in the Renaissance Revival style, is the only hotel building of its era that remains in the vicinity. It's now used as a shelter.

Rappahannock Apartments

16 Rappahannock (Rappannock) Apartments *L*

601–9 Ninth St. South

Lemuel Jepson, 1895

A good-sized apartment building notable for its fine wrought-iron balconies.

Heritage Apartments

17 Heritage (Mayhew) Apartments *L*

614–26 Ninth St. South

Frederick A. Clarke, 1886 / renovated, 1990

The oldest and most ornate building in the South Ninth Street Historic District, originally consisting of seven row houses. Early residents included the Reverend Marion Shutter, who wrote a three-volume history of Minneapolis published in 1923. Architect Frederick A. Clarke specialized in apartment buildings, including six others in this district. Later subdivided into 53 tiny apartments, this building was renovated around 1990. It now has 15 apartments.

18 William Lee Townhouse *L*

623–25 (possibly 619) Ninth St. South

William Channing Whitney, 1887 / 1894

The only Victorian-era townhouse left in either downtown Minneapolis or St. Paul. Fanciful ogee-arched windows on the top floor lend an Oriental air to the composition.

19 First Covenant Church (Swedish Tabernacle)

810 Seventh St. South

Warren H. Hayes, 1887 / addition (classrooms), 1937 / addition, ca. 1960s / restored, MacDonald and Mack Architects, 2004

This Romanesque Revival brick building looks more like a clubhouse or meeting hall than a traditional steepled church. Originally known as the Swedish

First Covenant Church

Tabernacle, it was built for a Scandinavian congregation founded in 1874. With an auditorium seating 2,500 people, it was among the largest churches of its time in Minneapolis.

20 Hennepin County Medical Center

701 Park Ave. South

Medical Facilities Associates General (Liebenberg Kaplan Glotter and Associates, S. G. Smiley and Associates, Thorsen and Thorshov Associates), 1975

General (or City) Hospital, as it was known, opened a block from here in 1887. By the early 1970s, the hospital was an almost incomprehensible jumble of buildings. Hennepin County, which had taken over the hospital in the 1960s, finally cleared away the old campus and in 1975 built this street-straddling behemoth.

Downtown East

Hennepin County Medical Center

It's not a pretty sight. Brutalist in style and spirit, the medical center walks on massive piers that look as though they could crush the ground beneath them, and it leaves a particularly unpleasant shadowland beneath its crossing on Seventh St. The layout is said to be highly efficient, but you have to wonder whether a hospital that seems to have been designed with the idea of scaring the hell out of patients is really a good thing.

21 Minneapolis Armory ! N

500–530 Sixth St. South

P. C. Bettenburg and Walter H. Wheeler (engineer), 1936 / Art: History of the National Guard (mural), Lucia Wiley, 1936 / Early Minnesota (mural), Elsa Jemne, 1936

A nationally significant example of the Moderne phase of art deco. With its graceful curves and gently rounded edges, the building doesn't quite convey the sense of jut-jawed militarism you'd expect from an armory, although it has an undeniably monumental presence. It's also something of an architectural Houdini, having escaped what looked to be certain destruction thanks to a court ruling in 1993. Unfortunately, surviving into architectural old age is no guarantee of a happy life, and today the armory is a parking garage.

The designer was St. Paul architect P. C. Bettenburg, who was also a major in the Minnesota National Guard. Bettenburg worked with Minneapolis engineer Walter Wheeler, who used a patented flat-slab concrete system for the large floor areas. The building has two sections: a drill hall on the Fifth St. side and four stories of offices overlooking Sixth St. Eight steel arches support the roof of the drill hall, which was also used for sporting events—the Minneapolis Lakers basketball team played here for a time—as well as concerts and other shows.

Virtually all of the building's exterior ornament—which includes a pair of stone eagles with 14-foot wing spans, bronze doors and screens, and Moderne-style lettering that spells out *Armory*—is concentrated around a pair of

Minneapolis Armory

entrances on Sixth. Within, the finishing is generally plain. However, an old trophy room still contains two Depression-era murals—*History of the National Guard* by Lucia Wiley and *Early Minnesota* by Elsa Jemne.

The armory's distinctive style is sometimes called PWA Moderne to denote its association with buildings constructed under the auspices of the Public Works Administration, a New Deal agency established in 1933. A PWA grant paid for about 20 percent of the armory's nearly $1 million construction cost, but most of the money came from the City of Minneapolis. In fact, the state didn't assume ownership of the armory until 1965.

The National Guard vacated the armory in 1983. Six years later Hennepin County purchased the building with the idea of razing it to make way for a new jail. However, the Minnesota Historical Society intervened and in 1993 won its case before the state's supreme court, which ruled that the armory was protected under a state environmental rights act. In 1998 Hennepin County, which later built its new jail elsewhere, sold the building to a developer who turned it into a parking garage. As part of the deal, the developer agreed to maintain the armory's historic appearance and to allow the county to use part of the site for a **Veterans Memorial Garden,** which opened in 2001.

LOST 1 Before the armory was built, this block was the site of the **William and Mary Judd House,** *constructed in about 1873 for a Minneapolis businessman and his wife. The Italian Villa–style house had a tall central tower and beautifully landscaped grounds. Later, the property functioned as a rooming house. It was torn down in 1926.*

22 People Serving People

614 Third St. South

Bertrand and Chamberlin, 1916 / renovated, Neil Weber Architects, 2002

A solemn old warehouse that now serves as an emergency shelter and temporary housing for homeless families. The Portland Ave. facade, which has brickwork arranged into large geometric patterns around small windows, is among the most distinctive of any warehouse in the city.

American Trio Lofts

23 American Trio Lofts (Northern Implement Co.) N *L*

616 Third St. South (also 250 Park Ave.)

Kees and Colburn, 1911 / renovated, ESG Architects, 2005

A fine brick warehouse building, now loft apartments, that shows the influence of at least three American architectural masters: Henry Hobson Richardson, Louis Sullivan, and John Wellborn Root, Jr. The broad top-floor arches and wide corner piers are modeled on Sullivan's Chicago warehouses, which in turn were inspired by Richardson's work in the Romanesque Revival style. Another distinctive feature—the subtle chamfer of the corners as they rise toward a flaring cornice—is derived from Root's 1891 Monadnock Building, which still stands in Chicago.

24 Thresher Square (Advance Thresher Co. Building, Emerson-Newton Plow Co.) N *L*

700–708 Third St. South

Kees and Colburn, 1900, 1904 / renovated, Arvid Elness Architects, 1984–86

A pair of beautifully misleading orange brick warehouses, built four years apart and seemingly identical until you look closely at their facades along Third St. The older of the two, originally constructed for the Advance Thresher Co., has six floors, while the adjoining Emerson-Newton Co. building has seven. However,

Thresher Square

these differing floor heights are so well disguised that the buildings, united under a common cornice, read as two halves of a single structure. Featuring swirling terra-cotta, they are clearly inspired by Louis Sullivan's work in Chicago, although the big terra-cotta cartouches pinned to the upper walls are actually Classical Revival in character. Both buildings, which have massive timber frames, were renovated into offices in the 1980s.

Downtown East/Metrodome Light Rail Station

25 Downtown East/Metrodome Light Rail Station, Plaza, and Parking Ramp

Kirby Puckett Pl. and Fifth St. South

HGA with Andrew Leicester (artist) and Philip Koski (artist), 2003

The light rail station here is tied in with a plaza that serves as a gathering spot in front of the Metrodome. The station and plaza include a series of colorful brick arches that pay homage to the Stone Arch Bridge a few blocks away. Patterns in the brickwork are intended to recall

those found in textiles worn by nineteenth-century immigrants in the Elliot Park neighborhood.

26 Hubert H. Humphrey Metrodome

900 Fifth St. South

SOM and others, 1982

A big beige bulge of a stadium everybody seems to hate even though it's worked quite nicely and at a cost that seems unbelievably low by the standards of today's absurdly expensive sports palaces. The Metrodome's billowing, air-supported fabric roof—a feature it shares with eight or so other large sports stadiums from the 1970s and 1980s—has been the subject of endless jokes, but it was in fact a good engineering solution to the problem of enclosing a large space at a reasonable cost. Two new stadiums (for the Twins and Gophers) have been built at a combined cost of over $800 million, while the Minnesota Vikings are lobbying for a new $1 billion home of their own. By comparison, the Metrodome was constructed for a mere $55 million.

The biggest criticism of the Metrodome has always been that it's a poor place to watch baseball, which is true. Yet it's also true that the dome's eccentricities—from its ultra-bouncy infield to its right field "baggy" to its occasionally deflated Teflon-coated roof into which baseballs can disappear like ships venturing into the Bermuda Triangle—have been responsible for many strange and memorable moments. There's also no doubt that the much maligned stadium was a critical factor in the Twins' two World Series victories, in 1987 and 1991, in which they won all of their home games.

While no one would ever mistake the dome for a thing of beauty, it could be argued that few other buildings ever constructed in the Twin Cities have delivered entertainment to so many at such a modest cost.

Hubert H. Humphrey Metrodome

27 Open Book Building

1011 Washington Ave. South

ca. 1900 / renovated, MS&R Architects, 2000

A handsome historic renovation by the architects of the nearby Mill City Museum.

28 Valspar Headquarters (Minnesota Linseed Oil Paint Co.)

1101 Third St. South

Long and Long, ca. 1904 and later / Art: Demolition *and* Sport *(murals), Peter Busa, 1974, 1982*

Colorful, abstract murals by artist Peter Busa add some diagonal gusto to an otherwise plain group of brick buildings that form the corporate headquarters of Valspar, a paint and coatings company. These were among the first large outdoor murals in the Twin Cities.

29 1010 Metrodome Square (Strutwear Knitting Co.)

1010 Seventh St. South

1922 / addition, Long and Thorshov, 1930 / renovated and enlarged, Setter Leach and Lindstrom, 1987

Now offices, this building with an art deco–style tower was built as a manufacturing plant for the Strutwear Knitting Co., which took its name from its owners, the Struthers family, and once employed as many as 1,100 workers. A bitter strike in 1935–36 closed the plant for months and at one point led Governor Floyd B. Olson to call out the National Guard.

30 Augustana Lutheran Church

704 11th Ave. South

William H. Dennis, 1883 / later additions

Founded by Swedish and Norwegian immigrants in 1866, this is one of several congregations with Scandinavian roots in Elliot Park. The church itself is a straightforward example of 1880s Gothic Revival, built of yellow brick. A number of additions have been made to the structure.

31 East Village Apartments

11th Ave. South between Eighth and 14th Sts. South

Miller Hanson Partners, 2001

A "new urbanist" project that's a cut above the usual work of this sort. The apartments and townhomes, 179 units in all, are nicely done, and a few shops are also part of the mix.

32 Professional Litho, Inc.

807 13th Ave. South

1906

A one-story building, constructed of yellow glazed brick with elegant terra-cotta trim. A ghost of a sign over the door identifies it as "Donaldson's," suggesting it may have been built as a garage for the department store of that name, long a fixture downtown.

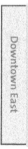

Downtown East

5 Loring Park

Loring Park

Situated at the edges of downtown, this urbane neighborhood offers an intriguing mix of old and new, the result of a complicated history of development, destruction, and renewal. Although the neighborhood's concentration of high- and low-rise apartment buildings makes it the densest residential precinct in the city, it still manages to be quite charming by virtue of the hilly topography at its southern end, its lovely old park, and its angled streets that happily ignore the domineering Minneapolis grid.

Loring Park's architectural diversity is extraordinary. Within its compact boundaries you'll find a 125-year-old park with its own lake, a modern greenway lined with apartments and townhomes, a scattering of Victorian and early twentieth-century mansions, a college campus, three of the city's most spectacular churches, and a historic commercial district that was once home to numerous auto-related businesses. It all calls to mind the kind of mixed-use neighborhoods found in Chicago or large East Coast cities, and there's nowhere else like it in Minneapolis or St. Paul.

First settled in the 1850s, the Loring Park area was initially the site of fairly modest homes but gradually evolved into one of the city's swankiest residential enclaves. Mansion building began in earnest in the 1880s after the opening of what was originally known as Central Park, renamed in 1890 to honor Charles Loring, first president of the Minneapolis Park Board. The park and its pond, the pleasing topography along the flanks of Loring Hill (part of the glacial ridge known farther to the west as Lowry Hill), and the neighborhood's proximity to downtown all appealed to wealthy homebuilders. Many of the largest mansions, such as the rock-ribbed Samuel Gale House (gone) of 1889, were built along Harmon Place on the park's north side. Apartment houses, including several that still stand north of Hennepin Avenue, also began appearing in the 1880s, a sign of things to come.

Loring Park's next great era of change occurred in the early twentieth century as commercial development fueled by the growing automotive business crept south from downtown. Today, the city's Harmon Place Historic District encompasses over 20 buildings that were once used to sell or service automobiles. This period also saw construction of the neighborhood's three landmark churches: St. Mark's Episcopal Cathedral (1911), the Basilica of St. Mary (1914), and Hennepin Avenue United Methodist Church (1916). Meanwhile, apartment buildings filled in the blocks around the park. By the 1920s, as autos and apartments continued to encroach, the neighborhood's historic mansions began to disappear, a trend that would continue for years to come. Today, virtually all of the neighborhood's surviving mansions are along the slopes of Loring Hill south of the park.

By the 1960s, the neighborhood, though not without a certain funky appeal, was at least partway down the road to seed and was losing population at a rapid clip. It was also being pinched in by construction of Interstate 94, which along with the later Interstate 394 cinches around the neighborhood like a thick concrete belt. The decline that became evident in the 1960s paved the way for redevelopment in the next decade. After much debate, the city in 1972 created the Loring Park Development District and empowered it with tax increments. Eventually, nearly 40 old buildings, mostly north and east of the park, were torn down to make way for new housing and institutional developments. The Loring Greenway (1976), linking Nicollet Mall to the park, was the new district's most notable public amenity.

Although the redevelopment project produced little in the way of memorable architecture, it did succeed in stemming the population decline and brought a new sense of vitality to the neighborhood.

Loring Park

POI A Loring Park !

1382 Willow St.

Horace Cleveland (landscape architect), 1883 / many later changes / renovated, Diana Balmori (New Haven, CT), 1996 / Art: Berger Fountain, Robert Woodward, 1975 / Ole Bull (bronze statue), Jacob Fjelde, 1897

The closest thing in downtown Minneapolis to a central park (in fact, that was once its name), even if it is well away from the main commercial core. Formally opened in 1883, the park is best known for its pond, which has two distinct bays linked by a narrow channel crossed by a pretty little bridge. Although the park has tennis courts, a playground, and other activity areas, it's primarily a passive green space and a pleasant one at that, despite the presence of Interstate 94 along its western edge. Keep an eye out for the park's squirrels, which may be the plumpest and most brazen in the Twin Cities. Artworks include the lovely, flowerlike Berger Fountain and Jacob Fjelde's statue of the Norwegian violinist Ole Bull.

1 Loring Park Community Arts Center (shelter)

1906 / renovated, Miller Dunwiddie Architects, 2003

Saved from demolition by neighborhood activists in the 1970s, this Mission Revival–style shelter now serves as a recreation and arts center for the Loring Park community.

2 Eitel Building City Apartments (Eitel Hospital)

1367 Willow St.

Long, Lamoreaux and Long, 1912 / renovated and enlarged, Loewenberg and Associates (Chicago) and BKV Group, 2008

An old medical complex turned into 211 apartments overlooking Loring Park. In 1912 Dr. George Eitel, a surgeon, built a hospital here that served a largely well-to-do clientele. Eitel also operated a clinic once located just across 14th St. The hospital was merged out of existence in the 1980s and later became a clinic. The complex now includes the renovated Classic Revival–style hospital building as well as a new addition.

3 Maryland Apartments (Hotel)

1346 LaSalle Ave.

Long and Long, 1907

A pleasant apartment hotel organized around a center court. At one time, four-story porches extended out from the two wings that face LaSalle.

4 Loring Greenway

Between Nicollet Mall and Loring Park

M. Paul Friedberg and Associates, 1976 / renovated, City of Minneapolis, 2008

This three-block-long pedestrian corridor, lined with townhomes and apartment towers, is one of the success stories of modern urban planning in Minneapolis. Designed as a centerpiece of the

Loring Park

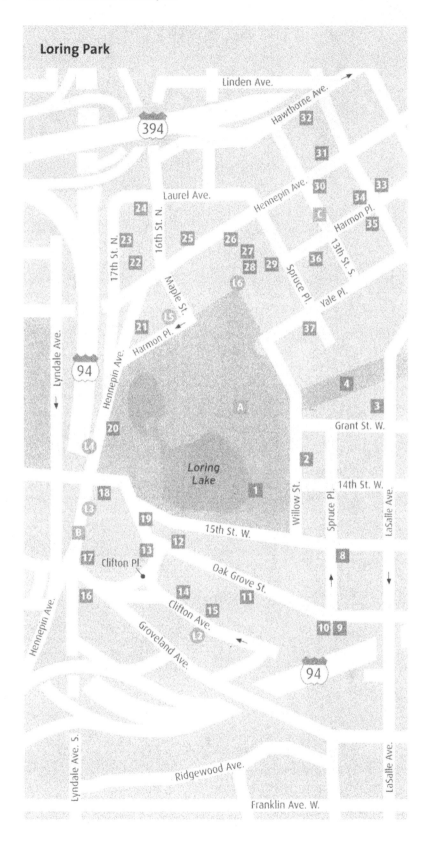

Loring Park

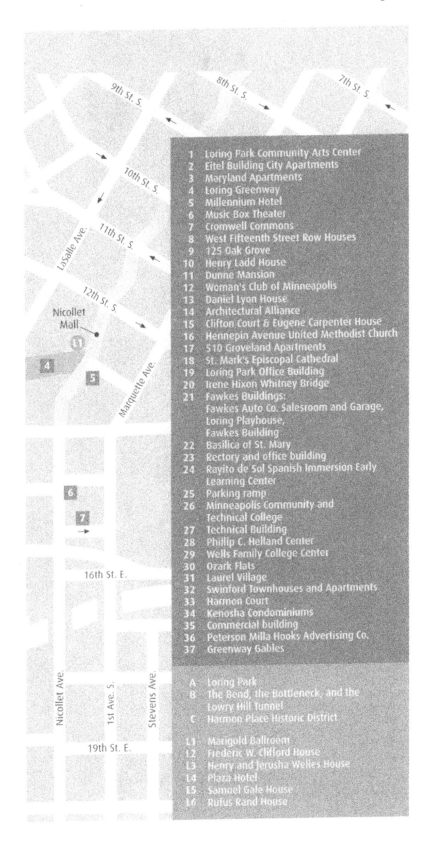

1   Loring Park Community Arts Center
2   Eitel Building City Apartments
3   Maryland Apartments
4   Loring Greenway
5   Millennium Hotel
6   Music Box Theater
7   Cromwell Commons
8   West Fifteenth Street Row Houses
9   125 Oak Grove
10 Henry Ladd House
11 Dunne Mansion
12 Woman's Club of Minneapolis
13 Daniel Lyon House
14 Architectural Alliance
15 Clifton Court & Eugene Carpenter House
16 Hennepin Avenue United Methodist Church
17 510 Groveland Apartments
18 St. Mark's Episcopal Cathedral
19 Loring Park Office Building
20 Irene Hixon Whitney Bridge
21 Fawkes Buildings:
    Fawkes Auto Co. Salesroom and Garage,
    Loring Playhouse,
    Fawkes Building
22 Basilica of St. Mary
23 Rectory and office building
24 Rayito de Sol Spanish Immersion Early
    Learning Center
25 Parking ramp
26 Minneapolis Community and
    Technical College
27 Technical Building
28 Phillip C. Helland Center
29 Wells Family College Center
30 Ozark Flats
31 Laurel Village
32 Swinford Townhouses and Apartments
33 Harmon Court
34 Kenosha Condominiums
35 Commercial building
36 Peterson Milla Hooks Advertising Co.
37 Greenway Gables

A   Loring Park
B   The Bend, the Bottleneck, and the
    Lowry Hill Tunnel
C   Harmon Place Historic District

L1 Marigold Ballroom
L2 Frederic W. Clifford House
L3 Henry and Jerusha Welles House
L4 Plaza Hotel
L5 Samuel Gale House
L6 Rufus Rand House

Loring Park

Loring Greenway

high-density residential community created here in the 1970s, the greenway functions both as a park for nearby apartment dwellers and as a pedestrian link between the Nicollet Mall and Loring Park. One reason the greenway works so well is that it's not a linear corridor but a picturesque sequence of spaces—some soft and green, others more hard edged—that create a sense of movement and variety. In 2007–8 the city renovated the greenway, which had begun to show its age, at a cost of $2 million. The work included adding more grass, planting a diverse array of new trees, and repairing the greenway's infrastructure.

LOST 1 *Where the Hyatt Regency Hotel now stands at 1300 Nicollet Mall was for over fifty years home to the* **Marigold Ballroom,** *a popular night spot that featured a 10,000-square-foot dance floor and attracted many big bands. The last dance occurred on May 26, 1975, after which the building was demolished.*

5 Millennium Hotel (Capp Towers)

1313 Nicollet Mall

Ackerberg and Cooperman, 1962 / renovated, 2000

A wonderful 1960s period piece, now remodeled in such regrettably good taste that it's lost its old, kitschy zing. Designed in a jazzy accordion-pleat shape, the hotel originally included a penthouse swimming pool and a domed rooftop cocktail lounge (now used for banquets and meetings). The building belongs to a family of flamboyant modernist hotels built in the 1950s

Millennium Hotel

and 1960s by such masters as Morris Lapidus in Miami and Wayne McAlister in Las Vegas.

6 Music Box (Loring) Theater

1407 Nicollet Ave.

Kees and Colburn, 1920 / renovated, Heise Vanney and Associates, 1986

An old movie theater turned playhouse that's gone through many lives, including a stint as a Pentecostal church. The brick and terra-cotta building features an arched parapet above a large rectangular window crowned by five decorative voussoirs.

7 Cromwell Commons

10 15th St. East

ca. 1892

A brick and brownstone apartment building with pointed Gothic arches rather than the round-headed variety you'd expect in the 1890s. Modern windows don't enhance the design.

8 West Fifteenth Street Row Houses *L*

115–29 15th St. West

Adam Lansing Dorr, 1886

The oldest row houses in the Loring Park neighborhood. Their general style is Romanesque Revival. The triple windows spanned by broad basket-handle arches include stained-glass transoms.

125 Oak Grove

9 125 Oak Grove (Bronzin Apartments)

125 Oak Grove St.

Alexander Rose, 1921

An impressive center-court apartment building, exceptionally well detailed in brick, glazed terracotta, and cast stone (a form of concrete). It was originally known as the Bronzin, a name created by combining those of its owners, Harry Zinman and Solomon Brochin. Note the blue and gold terra-cotta panels above the front windows, some of which sport fire-breathing dragons.

10 Henry Ladd House

131 Oak Grove St.

Harry Jones, 1889

Dark granite or brownstone was generally used for Richardsonian Romanesque mansions in the 1880s and 1890s, but here Harry Jones used golden Mankato-Kasota stone, with pleasing results. The wraparound porch, which features a gridiron-like stone

Henry Ladd House

railing, is particularly nice. The house's first owner, Henry Ladd, was in the real estate business.

11 Dunne Mansion (J. H. Lund House)

337 Oak Grove St.

Edward S. Stebbins, ca. 1893

An eclectic stone house, somewhere in the general vicinity of Romanesque Revival but with hints of Queen Anne in the shingles and half-timbering at the top of its steep gables. Built for a doctor and his wife, the house is now used for professional offices. Architect Edward Stebbins lived in a home nearby that was later moved to the Whittier neighborhood.

Woman's Club of Minneapolis

12 Woman's Club of Minneapolis

410 Oak Grove St.

Magney and Tusler (Leon Arnal), 1927

Founded in 1907 by some of the city's wealthiest women, this club has a diverse membership and remains known for its weekly programs that over the years have attracted everyone from Helen Keller to Frank Lloyd Wright. The Renaissance Revival–style club is attributed to French-born and -trained Leon Arnal, who worked in the 1920s and

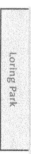

Loring Park

1930s for the local firm of Magney and Tusler.

13 Daniel Lyon House

419 Oak Grove St

Edward S. Stebbins, ca. 1892 / renovated, ca. 1994

A porticoed house built for a retired minister who favored a stovepipe hat and was said to bear an uncanny resemblance to Abraham Lincoln. The house is unusual in that its walls are of common Chaska brick, which wasn't normally used for mansions or on the main facades of buildings.

14 Architectural Alliance (Charles and Kate Bovey House) *L*

400 Clifton Ave.

Howard Van Doren Shaw (Chicago), 1916 / renovated, Architectural Alliance, 1984

A sedate brick house in the Federal variation of Colonial Revival and designed by a prominent Chicago architect. It was built for Charles Bovey, a vice president of the Washburn Crosby Co.

LOST 2 *Among the biggest of the mansions south of Loring Park was the* **Frederic W. Clifford House,** *at 325 Clifton Ave., where a modern apartment tower now stands. The huge Tudor Revival house, designed by Harry Jones, was built in 1905. Clifford was a founder of the Cream of Wheat Co. The house was torn down in 1968.*

15 Clifton Court (Elbert L. Carpenter House) *N L*

314 Clifton Ave.

William Channing Whitney, 1906 / renovated, ca. 1974

Eugene Carpenter House *N L*

300 Clifton Ave.

1890 / rebuilt, Edwin Hewitt, 1906

A pair of mansions originally owned by brothers. Perhaps the most "correct" example of the Federal Revival style in the Twin Cities, the Elbert Carpenter house

was built for an Illinois-born businessman who played a key role in establishing the Minneapolis Symphony (now Minnesota) Orchestra in 1903. Carpenter served as chairman of the orchestra's management committee

Eugene Carpenter House

and lived here for 40 years until his death in 1945. The house was converted to offices in the 1970s.

Eugene Carpenter's house began as a towered Queen Anne but was rebuilt in 1906, emerging from the process as a Georgian variation of Colonial Revival (and a good match for Elbert's mansion). Also an arts maven, Eugene was especially active on behalf of the Minneapolis Institute of Arts.

16 Hennepin Avenue United Methodist Church *!*

511 Groveland Ave.

Hewitt and Brown, 1916 / addition (education wing), McEnary and Krafft, 1950 / Art: stained-glass windows, Charles Connick (Boston), 1916 and later

At first glance this church, which overlooks Loring Park, appears to be very traditional, but it's actually a dynamic mix of elements old and new. The same can be said of its surroundings. Historic Loring Park spreads out to the north, but directly behind the church is the frenetic tangle of concrete that carries traffic over and through the Lowry Hill tunnel. The church feels a bit marooned in this setting, yet its proximity to the interstate also makes it one of the city's most-recognized buildings.

Although its general style is English Gothic—complete with traceried windows, buttresses, blind arcades, and a tower—the church is like nothing from the

Hennepin Avenue United Methodist Church

Middle Ages. Its stonework hides
steel, its centralized plan was
first used in nineteenth-century
Ohio, and its vaulted ceilings are
made with a type of interlocking
tile patented in 1885 by an architect from Spain. It is, in other
words, a characteristically American hybrid, and it's also one of
the city's great churches, rising in
craggy steps like a small moun-
tain and culminating in a needle-
thin, 238-foot-high spire that was
for a time among the tallest
structures in Minneapolis.

Hennepin Avenue Methodist
was formed in 1875 and occupied
a church at Tenth St. and Hennepin until 1911, when the congregation merged with the Fowler
Methodist Episcopal Church. In
need of a large new church, the
congregation settled on this site,
which was donated by Thomas
Walker, the lumberman and art
collector after whom the Walker
Art Center is named. Edwin

Hewitt, who'd just completed St.
Mark's Episcopal Cathedral a block
away, was hired to design the
new church. Born in Red Wing,

*Hennepin Avenue United Methodist
Church interior*

Hewitt was perhaps the best-
educated Minneapolis architect
of his time, with a résumé that
included a degree from the École
des Beaux-Arts in Paris.

The congregation's building committee instructed Hewitt and his partner (and brother-in-law), engineer Edwin Brown, to create a church that would look "ecclesiastical" (which meant Gothic) but would have an interior "in which the utilitarian should predominate." Hewitt proved up to the challenge. The church, built largely of stone from Vermont, does indeed look Gothic. Its plan, although inspired by an octagonal lantern built in 1322 at Ely Cathedral in England, isn't Gothic at all, however. Instead of a traditional nave, Hennepin Avenue Methodist has an Akron plan auditorium of the type favored by many Protestant congregations at the time. Creating a convincing Gothic church with a centralized plan was no small feat, but Hewitt managed it brilliantly. He employed another modern touch: the starburst vaulted ceiling is built of self-supporting Guastavino tiles, which bear the name of their inventor, Rafael Guastavino. The richly decorated interior also includes stained-glass windows designed by Charles Connick.

17 510 Groveland Apartments

510 Groveland Ave.

Larson and McLaren, 1927 / renovated, Bentz/Thompson/ Rietow Architects

A swank apartment building (now condominiums) that, with a few more stories and a more compact profile, could fit right in on Manhattan's Upper East Side. The T-shaped building, beautifully sited between Hennepin Avenue Methodist Church and St. Mark's Cathedral, is a generally restrained example of the Renaissance Revival style popular in the 1920s. Its boldest gesture is an outsized split pediment that presides over the front entrance.

POI B The Bend, the Bottleneck, and the Lowry Hill Tunnel

Hennepin Ave., Lyndale Ave., and I-94 tunnel, 1971

Before Interstate 94 was built, Hennepin crossed Lyndale Ave. here at an impossibly acute angle, producing the infamous "Bottleneck," a traffic free-for-all in which cars, trucks, and trolleys fought it out. Ideally, a freeway would never have been forced through this historic precinct, but there was no stopping highway builders and their vast pot of federal dollars in the 1960s and 1970s. The 1,500-foot-long Lowry Hill Tunnel, completed in 1971, does lessen the interstate's impact. Yet with so much surface traffic roaring along Hennepin and Lyndale, it's hard now to gain a sense of how Loring Park once related, visually and by means of connecting streets, to the Parade Grounds and Lowry Hill.

510 Groveland Apartments

St. Mark's Episcopal Cathedral

18 St. Mark's Episcopal Cathedral !

519 Oak Grove St.

Edwin Hewitt, 1908 (parish house), 1911 (cathedral) / addition (educational wing), Madsen and Wegleitner, 1958 / Art: stained glass, Charles Connick (Boston), 1918 / exterior sculptures, John Rood, 1952

The most traditional of the three large churches that overlook Loring Park. Architect Edwin Hewitt, who was an active member of the congregation, provided a faithful version of the English Gothic style. Its highlights include a tower modeled on that of Magdalen College at Oxford and a serene nave with plain brick walls, stone-clad columns, and a vaulted ceiling of Guastavino tile. It's said that Hewitt, a stickler for detail, even dressed in monk's robes while designing the church. Originally a parish church, St. Mark's was officially designated in 1941 as the cathedral of the Episcopal Diocese of Minnesota.

The church was built for what was at the time a fairly small Episcopal parish. Founded in 1868, St. Mark's completed its first per-manent church three years later on Sixth St. near Nicollet Ave. Plagued by debt, the parish had no real prospects for building a grand new church until a miracle of sorts occurred in 1905: an eastern real estate speculator offered the astounding sum of $275,000—over ten times the appraised value—for the old church and its land. The parish unaccountably stared this gift horse in the mouth for well over a year before finally accepting the offer, by then reduced to $250,000. After securing this prime site from the widow of a longtime church member, the parish—under the dynamic leadership of Bishop Samuel Cook Edsall—finally began construction here in 1907. The first services were held in the new church three years later.

Among St. Mark's greatest charms is its extensive sculptural program. Exterior sculpture by John Rood is concentrated above and around the main north doors. Rood's work includes a sculpture of Christ at the peak of the north facade, as well as figures of St. Mark and St. Peter. Within the archway around the doors Rood also carved 26 delightful bosses (knoblike projections) that depict Minnesota scenes.

There is more sculpture within, including an altar screen by Irving and Casson of Boston. The church's stained-glass windows are the work of, among others, Charles Connick, who also designed glass for Hennepin Avenue Methodist Church and the St. Paul Cathedral.

LOST 3 *The **Henry and Jerusha Welles House** once occupied the site of St. Mark's Cathedral and the 510 Groveland Apartments. Welles was a real estate dealer in the early days of Minneapolis. After his death in 1898, his widow sold the 30-room mansion to St. Mark's, and it was torn down to make way for the new church.*

19 Loring Park Office Building (Northwestern National Life Insurance Co.)

430 Oak Grove St.

Hewitt and Brown, 1924 / Art: murals (in lobby), Harry W. Rubins, ca. 1927

A refined office building originally constructed for a life insurance company. The wedge-shaped building features a monumental entrance in the form of a broad arch with low columned openings to either side, a motif much favored by Renaissance architects. It gives the building an elegant presence that you wouldn't typically associate with the prosaic business of selling insurance. Within, there are murals depicting early Minnesota and Minneapolis scenes.

20 Irene Hixon Whitney Bridge

Over I-94 at Loring Park

Siah Armajani, 1988

A multicolored pedestrian and bicycle bridge that crosses the 16 lanes of traffic separating Loring Park from the Walker Art Center and its sculpture garden. Armajani's design mimics both suspension and arch bridges, though in fact it's neither. If you undertake the crossing, make sure to read the poem by John Ashbery inscribed on the span's upper beams.

LOST 4 *The Whitney Bridge crosses the site of the **Plaza Hotel,** which once occupied a wedge of land between Hennepin and Lyndale Aves. at Kenwood Parkway. Built in 1906, the six-story brick hotel survived until 1960, when clearance began along the route of Interstate 94.*

21 Fawkes Buildings *L*

Fawkes Auto Co. Salesroom and Garage, 1625 Hennepin Ave.

Bell, Tyrie and Chapman, 1911

Loring Playhouse (Fawkes Auto Co.), 1629, 1633–37 Hennepin Ave.

Bell, Tyrie and Chapman, 1912

Fawkes Building, 1639–49 Hennepin Ave. (also 1620–24 Harmon Pl.)

Bell, Tyrie, Chapman and Gage (1645 Hennepin only), 1916–17

Restaurants, a theater, and other businesses now occupy these buildings, which are part of the Harmon Place Historic District. They were built for Leslie Fawkes, a pioneer auto dealer, and once included showrooms, offices, a warehouse, and a garage. The showpiece here is the Loring Playhouse, a former warehouse featuring a broad central window framed by bands of terracotta.

Samuel Gale House, 1900

LOST 5 *A fabulous mansion—the **Samuel Gale House**—once stood at Harmon Pl. and Maple St., just east of the Fawkes Buildings. Built in 1889 for a prominent real estate developer, the castlelike house was supposed to last for centuries. In fact, it was razed in 1933, a victim of the Depression and commercial encroachment.*

Basilica of St. Mary

22 Basilica (Pro-Cathedral) of St. Mary ! N i

1600 Hennepin Ave.

Emmanuel Masqueray, 1914 / interior, Slifer and Abrahamson, 1926 / restored and renovated, Miller Dunwiddie Architects, 1990s and later / Art: altar and baldachin, Maginnis and Walsh (Boston), ca. 1926 / stained glass, Gaytee Studios, ca. 1926

Overlooking Loring Park and Lowry Hill, the Basilica of St. Mary has perhaps the most majestic presence of any building in Minneapolis, and it is the city's outstanding monument from the age of Beaux-Arts classicism. It's also a grand Beaux-Arts companion piece to the even larger St. Paul Cathedral, designed by the same architect and built at the same time. Compared to the cathedral, the basilica is a more novel—if not necessarily superior—design, combining Renaissance, baroque, and neoclassical elements in a very peculiar way. It's also a more modern building than it appears to be, with heavy bones of steel beneath its stony skin.

The basilica's historic roots go back to the 1860s, when Immaculate Conception parish was established near Third St. and Third Ave. North. By 1900 the parish's old stone church was, in the words of one historian, "an oasis in a Sahara of warehouses." It was also too small, and in 1903 Archbishop John Ireland announced plans for a new church, which would also serve as a secondary cathedral (or pro-cathedral) for the archdiocese. In essence, Ireland had decided to build two cathedrals at once, a daunting proposition, especially when it came to finances.

Ireland, however, was a brilliant fundraiser and a most persuasive man. By 1905 he'd secured a site for the basilica on seven donated lots. He'd also found his

Basilica of St. Mary interior

architect: Emmanuel Masqueray. Ireland had met the French-born and -trained Masqueray in 1904 at the St. Louis World's Fair, where Masqueray was chief designer. Masqueray soon relocated his offices to St. Paul and began work on the cathedral there and the basilica here.

Masqueray adopted the broad, rectangular form of ancient basilicas here in part because money was an issue and he needed to keep the building relatively simple. As a result, the basilica resembles a huge decorated box, with two towers at one end and a 200-foot-high dome at the other. The dome, surmounted by a lantern, was originally supposed to have been round. It was later squared off (presumably to save money), a change that was actually for the better, giving it a distinctive profile.

Clad in white Vermont marble, the basilica is not a "correct" design in any historical sense. Instead, Masqueray stirred all manner of things into his architectural pot, from the Renaissance-inspired towers to a neoclassical Doric entry porch to three gigantic "telephone dial" windows (his trademark) that are actually nineteenth century in origin. Uniting it all is Masqueray's taste for bigness—he

was obviously an American at heart.

Within, the 82-foot-wide nave (two feet broader than that of St. Peter's in Rome) is spanned by a steel truss and girder system hidden above the barrel-vaulted plaster ceiling. The interior's lavish finishing dates to the 1920s. By that time Masqueray was dead, and the work was supervised by two former assistants, Frederick Slifer and Frank Abrahamson. As befitting its prominence, the basilica is loaded with artwork and fine furnishings. Of particular note are the marble altar and baldachin (canopy), wrought-iron grilles made by the Flour City Ornamental Iron Co., and numerous stained-glass windows by Thomas Gaytee of Gaytee Studios in Minneapolis.

The area around the basilica was drastically altered by the construction of Interstate 94. The heavy traffic created damaging vibrations, and by the 1980s age had also taken its toll on the church. The dome was in especially dire shape, leaking profusely during heavy storms. A renovation project began in 1991: workers disassembled and repaired the dome, then sheathed it in new copper. Other improvements included the installation of new bells and renovation of the undercroft (basement).

23 Rectory and office building

88 17th St. North

Slifer and Abrahamson, 1928

A three-story building, Georgian in character but with a steep French roof.

24 Rayito de Sol Spanish Immersion Early Learning Center (Basilica School)

1601 Laurel Ave.

Emmanuel Masqueray, 1913

A fairly simple brick building enlivened by a series of arched wall dormers. It was last used as a parish school in 1975.

25 Parking ramp

Hennepin Ave. at 16th St.

ca. 1970s / remodeled and enlarged, Bentz/Thompson/ Rietow Architects, 2005

A once drab college parking ramp spiffed up in 2005 with metal screens and some very cool lighting.

26 Minneapolis Community and Technical College (includes Minneapolis campus of Metropolitan State University)

1415 Hennepin Ave.

various architects, 1977 and later

Not the most charming college campus you'll ever see. It originally consisted of two separate institutions. The community college and the technical college were combined in 1996. Metropolitan State University relocated its Minneapolis campus here as well in 2004. Many of the campus's nine buildings are grouped around a fan-shaped plaza that overlooks Loring Park.

27 Technical Building

1415 Hennepin Ave.

Green Nelson Weaver and Winsor, 1977 / renovated, Bentz/ Thompson/Rietow Architects and Peterson Architects, 1993

The largest campus building and not a pretty one. The structure, clad mainly in striped bands of brick, was designed for energy efficiency—thus the glass panels facing the south—but the architects somehow neglected to make it even the least bit inviting.

28 Phillip C. Helland Center

Bentz/Thompson/Rietow Architects, 1986 / renovated, Cuningham Group, 2004

A purple brick building with dramatic triangular skylights facing toward the Technical Building.

29 Wells Family College Center (Alden Smith House) N L

1403 Harmon Pl.

William Channing Whitney, 1888 / renovated, 1996

The only surviving nineteenth-century mansion on Harmon

Phillip C. Helland Center, Minneapolis Community and Technical College

Wells Family College Center

Pl. Built of brownstone in the Richardsonian Romanesque style, it has a commanding corner tower ringed by small arched windows. Its first owner, Alden Smith, made his money in the sash and door business. Not surprisingly, there's much cherry woodwork inside. Used as a mortuary from 1919 until the 1970s, the house later became a restaurant before being acquired by the college in 1993.

LOST 6 *Among other mansions that once stood near here was the* **Rufus Rand House** *at 1526 Harmon. Like the Smith House, it was designed by William Channing Whitney but was Classical Revival in style. Built around 1890, it came down in the 1970s.*

30 Ozark Flats (Bellevue Hotel)

1225–29 Hennepin Ave.

William H. Grimshaw, 1893 / renovated, 1978

Now condominiums, this apartment hotel is linked to a famous murder. On the night of December 3, 1894, a 29-year-old seamstress named Kitty Ging who lived at the hotel was shot dead near Lake Calhoun. The murder was arranged by her lover, Harry Hayward, son of the hotel's owner as well as a gambler and a suave man about town. Hayward, who seems to have been a gold-plated psychopath, hired a none-too-swift janitor at the hotel to perform the actual killing. The motive was money—Hayward had taken out life insurance policies on Ging—though he also seems to have done it for a thrill.

Ozark Flats

Convicted of first-degree murder after a six-week-long trial, Hayward—dressed in a swallowtail coat and pin-striped trousers—was hanged on December 11, 1895, in the Hennepin County Jail. His last words to the hangman supposedly were, "Pull her tight. I'll stand pat."

31 Laurel Village

Hennepin Ave. between 11th and 14th Sts.

Winsor/Faricy Architects, Collaborative Design Group, and others, 1989–91

One of the first modern "urban villages" in the Twin Cities. It includes two apartment towers, townhomes, the historic Swinford complex, and a commercial-restaurant strip along Hennepin. The vaguely postmodern architecture isn't especially interesting.

Swinford Townhouses

32 Swinford Townhouses and Apartments (now part of Laurel Village) N L

1213–21, 1225 Hawthorne Ave.

Hodgson and Sons, 1886 (town-houses) / Harry Jones, 1897 (apartments) / both renovated, Bowers Bryan and Feidt, 1991

These buildings, located in what was once an upper-crust neighborhood near Hawthorne Park (1882, gone), are among the few deluxe urban apartments of their era that survive in Minneapolis.

The five three-story row houses offer an amalgam of classically derived styles—from French Second Empire to Renaissance Revival—done in red brick, brownstone, and terra-cotta. The Classical Revival–style apartment building designed a decade later by Harry Jones is even better. It's alive with distinctive details such

as the scrolled arch over the entrance and the bulbous corner bay. As built, the apartments had eight to 12 rooms; they have since been subdivided.

POI C Harmon Place Historic District L

Established in 2001 amid much controversy, this district encompasses around 25 buildings, most of which were constructed in the early twentieth century for the rapidly expanding automobile trade. In 2002 a state appeals court invalidated much of the district (which some property owners claimed had been created in an "arbitrary and capricious" manner). However, the Minnesota Supreme Court had the last word and ultimately upheld the city's original district boundaries.

Nothing in the district could be construed as a great work of architecture, but as a group the buildings show how designers of the era found ways to accommodate the novel requirements of the automobile in structures that were, by today's rude standards, remarkably urbane.

33 Harmon Court (Western Motor Supply Co. and Walter S. Milnor Garage) L

1128 Harmon Pl.

Jacob Stone, 1915

A crisp brick building that originally included an automotive

Swinford Apartments

parts firm and a separate repair garage.

34 Kenosha Condominiums (Flats) *L*

1204 Harmon Pl.

1907

This four-story brick building is typical of the apartments that began to appear near Loring Park early in the twentieth century.

35 Commercial building (Electric Carriage and Battery Co.) *L*

1207 Harmon Pl.

Purcell and Feick, 1911 / enlarged, HGA, ca. 1990

The oldest automotive building on Harmon Pl. Originally one story (the second floor is a modern addition), it was built for a company that sold electric cars, which in the early days of the automobile industry competed quite effectively with the gasoline-powered variety. The building, which once had decorative terra-cotta, is also significant as an early design by William Purcell, who soon teamed with

George Elmslie to form a partnership now renowned for its Prairie Style houses and banks.

36 Peterson Milla Hooks Advertising Co. (Oscar M. Nelson Co.) *L*

1315 Harmon Pl.

Carl B. Stravs, 1923

The district's most unusual building, its facade a carnival of patterned brick- and tilework. It was built as an automobile showroom and service garage. Architect Carl Stravs was born in what later became Yugoslavia and trained in Vienna. During his career in Minneapolis, which extended into the 1940s, Stravs produced a number of eccentric buildings, most notably the Phi Gamma Delta Fraternity House (1911) at the University of Minnesota.

37 Greenway Gables

Yale and Spruce Pls.

Bentz Thompson and Associates, 1979–80

Three-story townhomes, nicely designed in the postmodern mode of the time.

Annotated Bibliography

Adams, John S., and Barbara J. VanDrasek. *Minneapolis–St. Paul: People, Place and Public Life*. Minneapolis: University of Minnesota Press, 1993. Written by two geographers, this book provides a useful overview of the growth and development of the Twin Cities.

Anderson, David, ed. *Downtown: A History of Downtown Minneapolis and Downtown St. Paul in the Words of the People Who Lived It*. Minneapolis: Nodin Press, 2000. Good stories about the days when the two downtowns were truly at the center of life in the Twin Cities.

Atwater, Isaac, ed. *History of the City of Minneapolis, Minnesota*. New York: Munsell and Co., 1893. A big subscription book of the kind popular in the nineteenth century. It offers intriguing sketches of the city's white, overwhelmingly Protestant, and exclusively male establishment.

Bennett, Edward H., with Andrew Wright Crawford. *Plan of Minneapolis*. Minneapolis: Minneapolis Civic Commission, 1917. A grand Beaux-Arts plan for Minneapolis that never came to be. The plan's huge, dreamlike renderings are splendid.

Berman, James, ed. *St. Anthony Falls Rediscovered*. Minneapolis: Minneapolis Riverfront Development Coordination Board, 1980. An early survey of buildings in the St. Anthony Falls Historic District.

Besse, Kirk. *Show Houses, Twin Cities Style*. Minneapolis: Victoria Publications, 1997. A history of St. Paul and Minneapolis movie theaters.

Borchert, John R., David Gebhard, David Lanegran, and Judith A. Martin. *Legacy of Minneapolis: Preservation amid Change*. Minneapolis: Voyageur Press, 1983. A rather disorganized book that nonetheless contains much interesting information about the city's architecture and history.

Bromley, Edward A. *Minneapolis Portrait of the Past*. 1890. Reprint, Minneapolis: Voyageur Press, 1973. Wonderful photographs showing the city's earliest days.

Conforti, Michael, ed. *Art and Life on the Upper Mississippi, 1890–1915: Minnesota 1900*. Newark: University of Delaware Press, 1994. Includes chapters on turn-of-the-century Minnesota architecture and a long essay on the work of Purcell and Elmslie.

Diers, John W., and Aaron Isaacs. *Twin Cities by Trolley: The Streetcar Era in Minneapolis and St. Paul*. Minneapolis: University of Minnesota Press, 2007. The fullest account available of the streetcar system that helped shape almost every neighborhood in the Twin Cities.

Flanagan, Barbara. *Minneapolis*. New York: St. Martin's Press, 1973. The longtime newspaper columnist provides a breezy tour of her beloved Minneapolis. Fun to read, but don't rely on it for history lessons.

Gebhard, David, and Tom Martinson. *A Guide to the Architecture of Minnesota*. Minneapolis: University of Minnesota Press, 1977. Now badly dated, this remains the only comprehensive guide of its kind. The chapters on the Twin Cities omit many significant buildings, especially in St. Paul.

Hart, Joseph (with photographs by Edwin L. Hirschoff). *Down and Out: The Life and Death of Minneapolis' Skid Row*. Minneapolis: University of Minnesota Press, 2002. A well-written account of the old Gateway District, illustrated with elegant photographs.

Hofsommer, Don L. *Minneapolis and the Age of Railways*. Minneapolis: University of Minnesota Press, 2005. A comprehensive look at how railroads helped shape the growth of Minneapolis in the nineteenth and twentieth centuries. Well written and illustrated, but probably a bit too detailed for the general reader.

Hudson, Horace B., ed. *A Half Century in Minneapolis*. Minneapolis: Hudson Publishing Co., 1908. Yet another compilation, with some interesting stuff lurking amid the standard salutes to wealth and progress.

Jacob, Bernard, and Carol Morphew. *Pocket Architecture: A Walking Guide to the Architecture of Downtown Minneapolis and Downtown St. Paul*. 1984. Rev. ed., Minneapolis: AIA Minnesota, 1987. A decent but dull guidebook, now in need of much updating.

Kane, Lucile M. *The Falls of St. Anthony: The Waterfall that Built Minneapolis*. 1966. Rev. ed., St. Paul: Minnesota Historical Society Press, 1987. The definitive account of how the milling industry developed around St. Anthony Falls and turned Minneapolis into the world's leading flour producer.

Kenney, Dave. *Twin Cities Album: A Visual History*. St. Paul: Minnesota Historical Society Press, 2005. A nice array of photographs and other images that provide an overview of the history of Minneapolis and St. Paul. There's also an informative text.

———. *Twin Cities Picture Show: A Century of Moviegoing*. St. Paul: Minnesota Historical Society Press, 2007. Includes information on many old downtown theaters.

Kudalis, Eric, ed. *100 Places Plus 1: An Unofficial Architectural Survey of Favorite Minnesota Sites*. Minneapolis: AIA Minnesota, 1996. Various essayists describe their favorite buildings and places in Minnesota.

Larson, Paul Clifford, with Susan Brown, eds. *The Spirit of H. H. Richardson on the Midland Prairies: Regional Transformations of an Architectural Style*. Minneapolis and Ames: University of Minnesota Art Museum and Iowa State University Press, 1988. A series of essays examining the influence, in the Twin Cities and elsewhere, of the great Boston architect Henry Hobson Richardson.

Lathrop, Alan. *Churches of Minnesota: An Illustrated Guide*. Minneapolis: University of Minnesota Press, 2003. Includes information about a number of significant churches in the Twin Cities.

Martin, Judith, and Antony Goddard. *Past Choices / Present Landscapes: The Impact of Urban Renewal on the Twin Cities*. Minneapolis: Center for Urban and Regional Affairs, 1989. A straightforward account of how urban renewal dramatically altered St. Paul and Minneapolis.

McClure, Harlan E. *A Guide to the Architecture of the Twin Cities: Minneapolis and St. Paul, 1820–1955*. New York: Reinhold Publishing Co., 1955. Outdated, but interesting for its take on the first generation of "modern" architecture here.

Millett, Larry. *AIA Guide to the Twin Cities: The Essential Source on the Architecture of Minneapolis and St. Paul*. St. Paul: Minnesota Historical Society Press, 2007. Includes a lengthy chapter on downtown Minneapolis.

———. *Lost Twin Cities*. St. Paul: Minnesota Historical Society Press, 1992. A look at the Twin Cities' many vanished buildings.

Millett, Larry (with photographs by Jerry Mathiason). *Twin Cities Then and Now*. St. Paul: Minnesota Historical Society Press, 1996. Historic photographs of more than 70 street scenes paired with new pictures taken from the same locations.

Nord, Mary Ann, comp. *The National Register of Historic Places in Minnesota*. St. Paul: Minnesota Historical Society Press, 2003. Lists every Minnesota building on the register.

Olson, Russell L. *The Electric Railways of Minnesota*. Hopkins: Minnesota Transportation Museum, 1977. Written by a trolley buff, this study describes in sometimes numbing detail the Twin Cities' late, great streetcar system.

Orfield, Myron. *Metropolitics: A Regional Agenda for Community and Stability*. Washington, DC: Brookings Institution Press, 1997. A book about how to stem urban decline in St. Paul, Minneapolis, and elsewhere. Many interesting maps.

Pennefeather, Shannon M., ed. *Mill City: A Visual History of the Minneapolis Mill District*. St. Paul: Minnesota Historical Society Press, 2003. A handsomely illustrated book published to coincide with the opening of the new Mill City Museum.

Peterson, Richard, and Paul Clifford Larson. *Terra Cotta in the Twin Cities*. St. Paul: Northern Clay Center, 1993. A guide to buildings adorned with terra-cotta, which was widely used as an architectural material between 1880 and 1930.

Poppeliers, John C., S. Allen Chambers, Jr., and Nancy B. Schwartz. *What Style Is It? A Guide to American Architecture*. 1983. Rev. ed., Washington, DC: Preservation Press, ca. 2002. A useful guidebook that includes photographs, drawings, a glossary of terms, and a good bibliography.

Richards, Hanje. *Minneapolis–St. Paul Then and Now*. San Diego, CA: Thunder Bay Press, 2001. Lots of photographs, but the text isn't especially good.

Rosheim, David. *The Other Minneapolis, or the Rise and Fall of the Gateway, the Old Minneapolis Skid Row*. Maquoketa, IA: Andromeda Press, 1978. A fascinating look at a down-at-the-heels but historically significant part of Minneapolis destroyed by urban renewal in the 1960s.

Schmid, Calvin F. *Social Saga of Two Cities: An Ecological and Statistical Study of Social Trends in Minneapolis and St. Paul*. Minneapolis: Council of Social Agencies, Bureau of Social Research, 1937. Conceived as a Depression-era project, this is one of the most informative books ever written about the Twin Cities. Especially valuable are the superb maps and charts.

Schulyer, Montgomery. *American Architecture and Other Writings*. William H. Jordy and Ralph Coe, eds. Cambridge, MA: Harvard University Press, Belknap Press, 1961. Schuyler was an outstanding turn-of-the-century architecture critic. Includes a fascinating 1891 essay on buildings in St. Paul and Minneapolis.

Shutter, Marion D., ed. *History of Minneapolis, Gateway to the Northwest*. 3 vols. Chicago and Minneapolis: S. J. Clarke Publishing Co., 1923. This plump compendium, best taken in small doses, provides useful information about the city's early movers and shakers.

Stevens, John H. *Personal Recollections of Minnesota and Its People, and Early History of Minneapolis*. Minneapolis: Privately published, 1890. Stevens, who was among the first residents of Minneapolis, laid out the downtown street grid still in use today.

Stipanovich, Joseph. *City of Lakes: An Illustrated History of Minneapolis*. Woodland Hills, CA: Windsor Publications, 1982. The most recent full-dress history of the city and on the whole well done. Includes many photographs.

Torbert, Donald R. *Minneapolis Architecture and Architects, 1848–1908: A Study of Style Trends in Architecture in a Midwestern City Together with a Catalogue of Representative Buildings.* PhD diss., University of Minnesota, 1951. A good source of information about early Minneapolis architects.

———. *Significant Architecture in the History of Minneapolis.* Minneapolis: City Planning Commission, 1969. Torbert did pioneering research in local architectural history, but an extreme modernist bias often clouded his judgment.

Trimble, Steve. *In the Shadow of the City: A History of the Loring Park Neighborhood.* Minneapolis: Minneapolis Community College Foundation, 1989. A nicely written history of perhaps the most urbane neighborhood in Minneapolis.

Vandam, Elizabeth A. *Harry Wild Jones: American Architect.* Minneapolis: Nodin Press, 2008. A good survey of the work of Harry Jones, who designed a number of important buildings in downtown Minneapolis.

Westbrook, Nicolas, ed. *A Guide to the Industrial Archaeology of the Twin Cities.* St. Paul and Minneapolis: Society for Industrial Archaeology, 1983. Fascinated by bridges, dams, factories, railroad yards, and the like? If so, you'll enjoy this guide.

Writers' Program, Works Progress Administration. *Minneapolis: The Story of a City.* 1940. New York: AMS Press, 1948. A typical product of the Federal Writers Program sponsored by the Works Progress Administration.

Index

Every building and site described in the Guide is listed as a primary entry in the index, both by previous and current names. Building and street names beginning with numbers are alphabetized as if spelled out. The names of people, firms, organizations, and government offices involved in creating the works listed in the Guide appear in UPPER AND LOWER CASE SMALL CAPS. Unless otherwise indicated, they are architects, associated artists, or builders. Names of geographic areas or communities appear in *boldface italic*. A page reference in **boldface** indicates a photograph of the building, area, or other work.

The following abbreviations appear in the index:

Admin.	Administration	Co.	Company	Intl.	International
Amer.	American	Condos.	Condominiums	MN	Minnesota
Apts.	Apartments	Corp.	Corporation	Mpls.	Minneapolis
Assocs.	Associates	Ct.	Court	Natl.	National
Ave.	Avenue	Dept.	Department	RR	Railroad/Railway
Bldg.	Building	Hosp.	Hospital	St.	Street
Bros.	Brothers	Ins.	Insurance	Univ.	University

Picture Credits

Peyush Agarwal: 70 bottom

Rick Bronson: 13, 17, 20 top, 22 bottom, 23, 29 left and right, 32 bottom left, 33 top and bottom left and top right, 34 top, 36 bottom, 39 top and bottom right, 42 top, 43 left, 47 bottom, 50, 51 top, 52, 55 left, 56 bottom, 57 top, 59, 60, 61 left and right, 62, 63, 64 left and right, 68, 70 top, 71 top, 77, 78 bottom, 87 top, 88, 90 top, 91, 93, 100 bottom, 101 bottom right, 102, 104, 110 top

Diane D. Brown: 31 top, 37 bottom, 39 left, 47 top, 53 bottom, 97

Farrell photographic: 69 top, 79

George Heinrich: 54 left

HOK Sport: 57 bottom

Jazz Guy: 15 top

Bill Jolitz: 7, 12 top and bottom, 15 bottom, 18 bottom, 19 top, 20 bottom, 21 top and bottom, 22 top, 24, 25 top and bottom, 26, 28 left and right, 29 top, 35 left and

bottom, 38 bottom, 40, 43 right, 55 top and right, 56 top, 58 top and bottom, 71 bottom, 72, 76, 78 top, 87 bottom, 89 bottom, 90 bottom, 92 top, 100 top, 101 top right, 105, 110 bottom, 111 top and bottom

©Wayne Lorentz/CitiesArchitecture.com: 14 right, 69 bottom, 107

Frank Mazzocco: 16, 28 top, 34 bottom, 37 top, 42 bottom, 83, 86, 89 top, 92 bottom, 101 left, 103 top, 109

Colleen McGuire: 53 top

Minnesota Historical Society: 14 left, 18 top, 19 bottom, 30, 31 bottom, 32 right, 33 bottom right, 35 right, 41, 51 bottom, 54 right, 72, 73, 75, 103 bottom, 106, 108

Rick Neighbarger: 38 top

Bradley Nelson: 36 top

Ted Rolfes: 32 top left

Steve Schmeiser: 27

Maps by Map Hero—Matt Kania

Printed in the USA
CPSIA information can be obtained
at www.ICGtesting.com
JSHW060046150824
68134JS00031B/2651